COUNSELLING SKILLS FOR BECOMING A WISER PRACTITIONER

also in the Essential Skills for Counselling series

Counselling Skills for Working with Shame
Christiane Sanderson
ISBN 978 1 84905 562 8
eISBN 978 1 78450 001 6

Counselling Skills for Working with Trauma
Healing From Child Sexual Abuse, Sexual Violence and Domestic Abuse
Christiane Sanderson
ISBN 978 1 84905 326 6
eISBN 978 0 85700 743 8

of related interest

Practical Supervision
How to Become a Supervisor for the Helping Professions
Penny Henderson, Jim Holloway and Anthea Millar
Foreword by F. M. Inskipp
ISBN 978 1 84905 442 3
eISBN 978 0 85700 918 0

Neuroscience for Counsellors
Practical Applications for Counsellors, Therapists and Mental Health Practitioners
Rachal Zara Wilson
Illustrated by Pagan Tawhai
ISBN 978 1 84905 488 1
eISBN 978 0 85700 894 7

Ethical Maturity in the Helping Professions
Making Difficult Life and Work Decisions
Michael Carroll and Elisabeth Shaw
ISBN 978 1 84905 387 7
eISBN 978 0 85700 749 0

Theory and Practice of Focusing-Oriented Psychotherapy
Beyond the Talking Cure
Edited by Greg Madison
Foreword by Eugene Gendlin and Gene Gendlin
ISBN 978 1 84905 324 2
eISBN 978 0 85700 782 7

Self-Care for the Mental Health Practitioner
The Theory, Research, and Practice of Preventing and Addressing the Occupational Hazards of the Profession
Alfred J. Malinowski
ISBN 978 1 84905 992 3
eISBN 978 0 85700 931 9

COUNSELLING SKILLS FOR
BECOMING A WISER PRACTITIONER

Tools, Techniques and Reflections for Building Practice Wisdom

TONY EVANS
Foreword by Christiane Sanderson

Jessica Kingsley *Publishers*
London and Philadelphia

First published in 2015
by Jessica Kingsley Publishers
73 Collier Street
London N1 9BE, UK
and
400 Market Street, Suite 400
Philadelphia, PA 19106, USA

www.jkp.com

Copyright © Tony Evans 2015
Foreword copyright © Christiane Sanderson 2015

All rights reserved. No part of this publication may be reproduced in any material form (including photocopying or storing it in any medium by electronic means and whether or not transiently or incidentally to some other use of this publication) without the written permission of the copyright owner except in accordance with the provisions of the Copyright, Designs and Patents Act 1988 or under the terms of a licence issued by the Copyright Licensing Agency Ltd, Saffron House, 6–10 Kirby Street, London EC1N 8TS.

Applications for the copyright owner's written permission to reproduce any part of this publication should be addressed to the publisher.

Warning: The doing of an unauthorised act in relation to a copyright work may result in both a civil claim for damages and criminal prosecution.

Library of Congress Cataloging in Publication Data
Evans, Tony (Counseling psychologist)
Counselling skills for becoming a wise practitioner :
tools, techniques and reflections for building
practice wisdom / Tony Evans.
pages cm
Includes bibliographical references.
ISBN 978-1-84905-607-6 (alk. paper)
1. Counseling psychology. 2. Counseling psychologist
and client. 3. Psychotherapy. 4. Counseling. I.
Title.
BF636.6.E92 2015
158.3--dc23
2014047771

British Library Cataloguing in Publication Data
A CIP catalogue record for this book is available from the British Library

ISBN 978 1 84905 607 6
eISBN 978 1 78450 143 3

Printed and bound in the United States

Dedicated to LB

CONTENTS

Series Editor's Foreword by Christiane Sanderson — 9

    ACKNOWLEDGEMENTS — 11

Part 1 Introduction to Becoming a Wiser Practitioner — 13

Part 2 The Streams of Practice Wisdom — 37

1. Hovering on the Edge — 40
   - Stream 1: The Leap of Faith — 43
   - Stream 2: Discovery — 48
   - Stream 3: The Journey — 53
   - Stream 4: Adventure — 58

2. Jumping In — 63
   - Stream 5: Play and Exploration — 65
   - Stream 6: Inner Child — 70
   - Stream 7: Slowing Down — 80
   - Stream 8: Story and Metaphor — 85
   - Stream 9: Dialogue — 91
   - Stream 10: Space and Place — 95

3. Diving Deeper — 100
   - Stream 11: Seeing, Listening, Feeling — 102
   - Stream 12: Embodiment — 107
   - Stream 13: Immersion — 111
   - Stream 14: Intuition — 116
   - Stream 15: Empathy — 120

	Stream 16: Tacit Knowledge	125
	Stream 17: Humour	129
	Stream 18: Warmth	134
4	Special Equipment	138
	Stream 19: Juggling	140
	Stream 20: Improvisation	145
	Stream 21: Digging	149
	Stream 22: Intersubjectivity	155
	Stream 23: Presence	160
	Stream 24: Bravery	164
	Stream 25: Creativity	170
5	Rip Tides	175
	Stream 26: Struggle	177
	Stream 27: Balance	184
	Stream 28: Wholeness	189
	Stream 29: Power	194
	Stream 30: Morality	198
	Stream 31: Difference	202
	Stream 32: Complexity	206
6	Practised Wisdom	213
	Stream 33: Maturity	214
	Stream 34: Craftsmanship	221
	REFERENCES	231
	SUBJECT INDEX	234
	AUTHOR INDEX	238

SERIES EDITOR'S FOREWORD

The landscape of therapeutic practice is a constantly changing terrain that reflects current mental health concerns and increasingly diverse client populations. This, along with keeping up to date with the latest research in the field of mental health and good practice, poses considerable challenges for practitioners as they try to balance the demands of their practice with continuous professional development. The Essential Skills for Counselling series is designed to provide clinicians, therapists, counsellors, health professionals, social care practitioners, and trainees with a range of tried and tested skills to enable them to enhance their practice. The emphasis is on exploring current changes in knowledge and practice which can be incorporated into their existing practice and theoretical model or orientation. The books in the series will focus on skills and techniques that are particularly useful when working either with particular client groups, such as survivors of childhood sexual abuse, or specific presenting symptoms such as complex trauma or shame.

Many practitioners are not always able to keep abreast of the latest research or be familiar with developments in practice and range of therapeutic techniques across different modalities. The handbooks in this series aim to provide current knowledge in working with particular client groups or specific mental health issues that practitioners may not have encountered in their original training. To enhance awareness and understanding the books will encourage practitioners to challenge their own perceptions and practice through self-reflection and a series of tried and tested exercises that they are invited to engage with and which can be used with clients.

The books in the series will be user friendly, using clear, accessible and easy to understand language with icons to signpost important points and good practice points. There will be boxes for experiential exercises and skills and exercises to use with clients. Practitioners will be able to dip in and out of the books as they need to, enabling them to access relevant information and skills without having to read extensively. To enliven the text case examples will be included to show how the skills can be employed. The focus throughout is on clear and succinct descriptions of skills, how they can best be employed and making the practitioner more aware of their own process in their work, enabling them to become more sentient practitioners.

Tony Evans' book is the latest addition to the series reflecting the timely paradigm shift seen in current affective neuroscience that emphasises the role of implicit, non-conscious processes that allow for the right-brain to right-brain therapeutic practice at the heart of human experience. The aim of the book is to fill the gaps between theory and practice allowing for deeper change during psychotherapy. It explores what happens to theory when it meets real life and how individuals and practitioners learn mainly from experience and from doing. In this it conveys the reality of the counselling room and provides helpful tips and techniques to enable practitioners to develop and refine their ability to enter into another person's internal world, thereby gaining practice wisdom.

At the heart of this book is the idea of 'situated' action in which purely intellectual faculties are suspended to allow for a different kind of intelligence – one shaped in the real world during down-on-the-ground, embodied and deeply felt experiences. Through a mixture of reflection, client stories, quotes, metaphor and visual images it explores right-brain affective processes such as warmth, embodiment, intuition, imagination, creativity, play, humour, empathy, presence, balance, intersubjectivity, maturity and craftsmanship, and how these are fundamental to change and growth and developing wisdom. The book, while primarily aimed at anybody training in the helping professions (counsellors, psychotherapists, psychologists, arts and play therapists, teachers), will also be a source of inspiration and reflection for the experienced, seasoned practitioner wanting to reflect on their process and develop their skills.

Christiane Sanderson 2015

ACKNOWLEDGEMENTS

I would firstly like to acknowledge Dr Jamie Moran who originated and developed the Reflective Practice course at University of Roehampton and contributed much to the thinking and discussion behind the material in this book. Secondly, Matthew Trustman who teaches with me on the course and wrote the majority of the Space and Place and Embodiment streams. Thirdly, my ever supportive and creative colleagues Chrissie Sanderson (who also acts as the series editor for this book), Jo Cruywagen and Nicole Proia, who teach on Reflective Practice and my fantastic Head of Department, Dr Diane Bray.

I must also acknowledge the many clients, students, supervisors and supervisees who have helped me to develop my thinking around situated action. Without my dynamic dialogues and relationships with them this material would not have fully developed.

Personally I have relied on the support over many years of my dear friends and the siblings that I never had: Doug Osborne, Claire Scott, Yuri Yushchuk, and those who have been both friends and valued professional colleagues, Dr Jean O'Callaghan, Gillie Sliz, Belinda Round-Turner and Susan Peacock, and my parents Joan and David Evans.

Part 1

INTRODUCTION TO BECOMING A WISER PRACTITIONER

> Science is organised knowledge, wisdom is organised life.
>
> Immanuel Kant

Most of us have largely been schooled in the Western educational tradition of acquiring bodies of knowledge, applying them to problems and to finessing a critical, analytic eye to be applied to the claims of science, research and argument. When training as therapists, counsellors and counselling psychologists we are introduced to the various models of psychotherapeutic practice – from Freudian and Kleinian, through object relations, to cognitive-behavioural therapy (CBT), humanistic and existential – and gradually learn to employ one or more of these academically informed approaches to understanding the aetiology and maintenance of human psychological distress and how we might go about trying to relieve it as practising therapists.

The approach this book champions invites practitioners to temporarily suspend these purely intellectual and abstract faculties and to begin exploring a different kind of intelligence – one shaped in the real world during down-on-the-ground, embodied and deeply felt experiences – to explore what happens to theory when it meets real life. Many therapists struggle to let go of the models-led theoretical approaches at first, dominated by fears of failure, anxieties about being out of their depth and sturdy conviction that the books, the research, the theories – *the others* – must know best. This is wholly understandable given that most of us have been trained to think this way since early childhood.

In exploring how to become a wiser practitioner my starting point is that people learn mainly from experience and from doing, that people encountering real life phenomena in the field gain something valuable they cannot acquire in purely academic settings or via cognitive, abstract processes. The body and the heart need to learn too. Real expertise, competence, even mastery, never come from slavish obedience to the dictates of a theory, but depend crucially on the way in which the practitioner refines and improves their 'situatedness' with reality. Many practitioners think of it as *situated action*: a term first coined by Professor Lucy Suchman in her 1987 book about human–computer interaction. Perhaps the oldest labels for such experiential learning are from philosophy: *Praxis* and *Phronesis*. The notion of *praxis* is ancient and has been considered by Plato and Aristotle, as well as St Augustine, Immanuel Kant and Sigmund Freud. It is concerned with the realities of applying abstract ideas in the real, grounded field of the world. What happens in the relationship between theory and practice? Aristotle (1962 [4 BC]) felt that the end product of *praxis* should be action – action that is embedded and embodied in real-world territory. He saw it as a radically different form of knowing from *theoria* (theory) which was aiming to find 'truth'. Hannah Arendt, in *The Human Condition* (1958) offered a critique of Western philosophy as having become too contemplative, too far removed from real active living. She saw *praxis* as a 'mode of human togetherness…participatory democracy which stands in direct contrast to the bureaucratised and elitist forms of politics so characteristic of the modern epoch'. This is a powerful evocation of what the best therapeutic relationships can do – we practitioners are rarely at our best when strangled by bureaucracy and rigid rule following; they can cause us to lose sight of the humanity of the person we are working with and to lose touch with our own innate creativity, intuition and emotional responsiveness.

Aristotle in Book VI: Intellectual Virtue of his *Nicomachean Ethics* (1953 [4 BC]) goes on to distinguish between *sophia* (theoretical wisdom) and *phronesis* (practical wisdom):

although the young may be experts in geometry and mathematics and similar branches of knowledge [*sophoi*], we do not consider that a young man can have Prudence [*phronimos*]. The reason is that Prudence [*phronesis*] includes a knowledge of particular facts, and this is derived from experience, which a young man does not possess; *for experience is the fruit of years* [emphasis added]. (p.124)

To honour *praxis* and develop *phronesis* in our students my colleagues and I teach a Reflective Practice module, where students begin the never-ending, exciting, frightening and empowering process of coming to trust their own intuitive, experientially acquired knowledge – and developing a sceptical, questioning and critical eye towards therapy models and their implicit claims about how the real world operates. We[1] help them to understand that this way of moving from the apprentice state towards craftsmanship – in any field – is ancient, celebrated and understood across cultures and across time.

Intelligence alone is not enough for acting wisely.

Fyodor Dostoevsky

THE 10,000 HOURS – OR THE 10-YEAR RULE

Malcolm Gladwell in his book *Outliers: The Story of Success* (2009) tries to work out what factors contribute to exceptional attainment in any field. Historically people have suggested natural talent, genetic inheritance, even divine intervention as explanations for exceptional achievement. His main answer to this question is something far more prosaic – extraordinary amounts of practice in the field – something approaching 10,000 hours. Examining the development of expertise in chess, Simon and Chase (1973) found that no one reached the level of international chess master (grandmaster) 'with less than about a decade's intense preparation with the game' (p.402) – roughly 1000 hours of operating within the field of chess for each of the ten years.

Anders Ericsson, Krampe and Tesch-Romer (1993) looked at the journey of those training to be violinists at the Music Academy in West Berlin. They found that those considered to be elite players had engaged in about 10,000 hours of practice since they first picked up a violin;

---

1 Wherever 'we' or 'our' is used in discussing work with students on the Reflective Practice programme I am referring to myself and my colleagues.

those ranked as less able players about 4000. One might expect that certain 'natural stars' would be able to shortcut this long process and reach mastery much more rapidly. Interestingly they did not find this: there were no real shortcuts and less truth than commonly supposed in the idea that natural ability will always shine through. Continual practice over a long period of time seemed to be the key to achieving brilliance and reaching the elite ranks of violin players.

Robert Greene in his recent book *Mastery* (2012), which topped the *New York Times* bestseller list, defines the elements that explain why so few human beings reach a genuine stage of mastery in life. He argues that one necessary dimension is spending much time in the 'apprentice stage', analogous to the 10,000 hours.

> The principle is simple and must be engraved deeply in your mind: the goal of an apprenticeship is not money, a good position, a title, or a diploma, but rather the transformation of your mind and character – the first transformation on the way to mastery. You enter a career as an outsider. You are naïve and full of misconceptions about this new world. Your head is full of dreams and fantasies about the future. Your knowledge of the world is subjective, based on emotions, insecurities, and limited experience. Slowly, you will ground yourself in reality, in the objective world represented by the knowledge and skills that make people successful in it. You will learn how to work with others and handle criticism. In the process you will transform yourself from someone who is impatient and scattered into someone who is disciplined and focused, with a mind that can handle complexity. In the end, you will master yourself and all of your weaknesses. (p.65)

This long journey toward mastery has been recognised world-wide in very different cultures for thousands of years: various forms of apprenticeship were seen in ancient Egypt, Greece and Rome and had to be completed in order to enter many of the trades, professions and crafts. Versions of this set-up existed in ancient China, India, in the guilds of the Muslim nations. Whether it was the training of shamen in Korea, goldsmiths in Venice, classical gardeners in Japan or stonemasons in Medieval London there was an old, well-understood path for those entering the field to follow. A period of apprenticeship to a master craftsman (often around the seven-year mark, starting at maybe 13 or 14 years of age), was followed by a period as a journeyman, usually employed on a daily basis for simpler jobs, and eventually upon demonstration of your skills, knowledge and ability in your field admittance to a guild as a master craftsman in your own right. Some guilds required you to produce a 'masterpiece' of your own as the price of entry to their closed world. In this way the traditions of the craft were passed on to the next generation and the professional standards of the profession were maintained. This framework was tested and proved across many decades, centuries and millennia all over the world. To return briefly to Aristotle: 'the moral virtues we do acquire by first exercising them. The same is true of the arts and crafts in general. The craftsman has to learn how to make things, but he learns in the process of making them. So men become builders by building, harp players by playing the harp' (1953, p.56)...and of course we become therapists by 'therapising'. Repeated embodied experience is the seat of becoming that which we wish to become.

However it is true to say that *this way* – the slow and purposeful building of practical wisdom – is becoming increasingly drowned out in the modern fields of education, training and, for our particular purposes, the training of counsellors, psychotherapists and counselling/clinical psychologists, where form filling, funding worries, top down bureaucratic control and rigid models-led training hamper the individual's gathering of practice wisdom. The aim of this book is to make a small contribution to the restoring of balance and to offer some insights gleaned from time spent walking on the road. In many trainings today the number of client hours needed to qualify is ever shorter, the time spent in personal therapy and supervision cut, the length of the training programme itself squeezed – meanwhile the student's expectations and fantasies about how one obtains a state of mastery seem to demand faster, easier, simpler routes with which providers feel pressured to comply. In such environments it is no wonder that the slow acquisition of lived skill needed to practise well can be skimmed over. The modern world does not help, addicted as it is to immediacy, novelty, intensity and speed, with ever more complex technology replacing more and more human interaction. Taken together all these forces only exacerbate the natural tendency of younger humans, uncomfortable with any sense of waiting, of rushing too fast towards the destination and missing most of the ride.

The book is aimed at all of us travelling from apprenticeship to mastery – wherever we happen to be on the journey right now. It encourages us to slow down and pay greater attention to the ancient sense of progression towards master practice. There was – and is – great wisdom built into that framework which is why it survived for so long. I imagine this work is likely to be of interest to students of counselling, psychotherapy and psychology, those who teach and supervise them, and to those already practising – be it for one year or 40. The same principles apply to any journey towards craftsmanship and wisdom – it is not unique to therapy. The substantial elements of this book are set out as essential 'streams' of practice wisdom. They represent the skills, knowledge, experiential awareness, personal qualities and existential attitudes which typify both the better sort of student and the highest forms of mastery in practice. The streams are an attempt to deconstruct practice wisdom out of the field and give shape on the page to something primarily lived down on the ground.

Many of the university students I have taught this material to find the streams as relevant to their wider life as to the part of it specific to therapy – I hope you will too. The best therapists naturally apply the wisdom of living to their work – there should be no artificial separation. Each of the 34 streams of practice wisdom contains a mixture of reflections, client stories, associated knowledge, and ideas for the practical application of skills, quotes, images and excerpts from students' writing. Each stream has a 'Reflection Point' box with some ideas about how the stream might show up in your non-therapeutic life and a 'Streams in the Consulting Room' box, which explores how the stream may manifest subtly in therapy space and how to engage with it when it does.

In developing practice wisdom the journey never truly ends until we do.

A FIRST DIP IN THE WATER

Rumi (1207–1273), the Persian Sufi poet, argues that there are two kinds of intelligence, different as chalk and cheese. Rumi's claim is central to this book.

> There are two kinds of intelligence: one acquired,
> as a child in school memorises facts and concepts
> from books and from what the teacher says,
> collecting information from the traditional sciences
> as well as from the new sciences.
> With such intelligence you rise in the world.
> You get ranked ahead or behind others

> in regard to your competence in retaining
> information. You stroll with this intelligence
> in and out of fields of knowledge, getting always more
> marks on your preserving tablets.
> There is another kind of tablet, one
> already completed and preserved inside you.
> A spring overflowing its springbox. A freshness
> in the center of the chest. This other intelligence
> does not turn yellow or stagnate. It's fluid,
> and it doesn't move from outside to inside
> through the conduits of plumbing-learning.
> This second knowing is a fountainhead
> from within you, moving out.
>
> (From *The Essential Rumi*, trans. C. Barks, 1995, p.178)

The container for the intelligence that Rumi metaphorically describes as a fountainhead I have come to refer to as 'The Well'. Years ago during my clinical training, when I would worry excessively about whether I was doing therapy 'properly', I realised that no matter how scared, self-conscious or blocked I was feeling just before I stepped in to see a client – something happened to me once I was inside the space. Things – feelings, thoughts, words, images, bits of theoretical models, bodily sensations, flashes of intuition – just seemed to 'show up' when I needed them. It felt almost like an empty bucket going down into a well – coming back to the surface full of water. Gradually, when I felt that stab of anticipatory anxiety about my therapeutic skills, especially right before exams, supervision sessions or seeing clients, I learned to say to myself, 'Don't worry, the bucket is empty now – but the well is getting fuller every day.' Every book I read, every lecture I heard, conversations with colleagues and mentors, every client session and its accompanying note taking, each log in my reflective journal was continuing to fill a well that was already more plentiful than I had ever realised (after all I had lived 30 years in this world before I came to study psychology). The key for me was to trust the existence of the well of practical wisdom inside me and to know it was there when I needed it.

The well is inside every person, and operates as a holder and delivery mechanism for an intelligence which is concrete and grounded, rather than abstract and theoretical. What the modern Western education system now calls intelligence is sometimes limited to cleverness and calculation, built out of facts, theories, proof and scientific evidence. From a young age we are encouraged to value such knowledge – and the intelligence required to understand and reproduce it – as the only true form of intelligence needed in the world. Wisdom developed from doing, from feeling, seeing, listening, imagining and living tends to be under-valued – at various times in the past 300 years it has been categorised as being more native or primitive, more female, more childlike or more working class. The elevated ways of understanding the world have come to be those understood as more Western, more scientific and more male. They are viewed as firmly adult and dominated by the educated and economically powerful classes who then pass this life approach to their own children. It is important to be clear from the outset that this book is not attempting to jettison scientific research and its associated discoveries. To do so would be foolish. However I am proposing that this abstract way of knowing about and being in the world tends to become ever more removed from down-on-the-ground practice over time. It can become overly concerned with categories, measurement, targeting and proving one side right and the other wrong. It certainly tends to devalue wisdom acquired mainly from practice in real-world territory. Put simply it values the map far more than the terrain.

It is useful for 'mind-obsessed' Westerners to realise that the kind of intelligence they revere, and is increasingly built into their institutions, is not geared to respond to the here and now, the particular, the shifting sands over which people actually have to walk. To help one travel through the forest or the desert, a map of the place is not enough – as many have discovered to their cost. A human guide that really knows the territory has access to many forms of knowledge that can never be scribed onto paper and they have usually developed them over time during repeated visits to the same terrain. They have been tested by it, schooled by it, come to know it. I would argue that any walk of life is much the same – and that the same thing applies to the practice of therapy. Thus, situated – as opposed to abstract – intelligence is, by definition, 'practical'. This takes us precisely back to the outline of *phronesis* from Aristotle discussed previously.

> In study after study it has been shown that no particular…therapy model proves itself more or less…than any other. The obvious conclusion from this is that theory is not the key ingredient to effective practice. It is far more likely that the crucial factor is something highly personal [in] what [a therapist knows] about himself or herself

> and the client, and the present happening between the two, which is the creative factor. This has…been referred to as 'practice wisdom'.
> (Altheide and Johnson 1994, p.488)

We encourage students to critically question the claim that theory always drives practice. Indeed, we have reached the conclusion that there is a kind of theorising which, in fact, positively blocks the effective practice of any complex activity, such as a way of life, a vocational calling, or even a relatively straightforward skill.

People too wedded to theory do not make effective practitioners. They may be able to talk the walk, and this sounds very impressive, but when it comes to actually walking the walk, they turn out to be clumsy, ponderous, inflexible, and thus ineffectual. People tend to neglect how often theory fails to work out in practice, and they avoid asking why this might be so. Instead, they search for another, better theory – how to build a better mousetrap.

If theory is poorly placed to teach us about reality, then the alternative is to learn directly from reality itself. The practitioner's focus is on the actual terrain where their activity takes place, not on the theory in their head. I will therefore speak of the 'situated practitioner'. The alternative to practice being driven by abstract theory is practice being driven by the concrete situation.

However, caution is needed here – situatedness is not a matter of overturning the clarity and discipline of theory just to indulge the emotive or the anarchistic. We cannot move well on the ground by relying on superstition, prejudice, opinion or self-indulgence, and 'anything goes'. Situatedness is a process with its own ethos and dynamic, and its own discipline. In our teaching we encourage students to begin experiencing this process for themselves and this book invites you to do the same – no matter how long you have been practising already.

> The therapeutic encounter, like any intimate relationship, is full of mystery, surprise and unpredictable turns. No matter how well trained in therapy [theory] and technique, the encounter with another human being who seeks relief from suffering invariably challenges them [the therapist] in ways that their training has not prepared them for.
> (O'Leary 1995, p.54)

Models-led cognition and action is top-heavy with anticipated knowledge of and anticipated control over situations. Situated action accepts that real-world contexts are not predictable and not controllable in any straightforward sense. We do not and cannot know in advance how really 'the land lies' and what might be an appropriate reaction to 'prevailing conditions'. Such knowledge must be discovered in the situation, by a certain way of opening up to and wrestling with it, and thus action is always exploratory, and constantly being revised.

Situated action challenges long-standing 'rationalist myths' (models-led claims) about human intelligence	
Models-Led Claim	**Situated-Action Reply**
Theory is superior to practice	Practice beats theory in real-world knowledge
Theory rises above the mess and complexity of reality	Intelligent action doesn't always need maps
Theory provides blueprints for executing action	Insight can be generated in the moment
Action cannot function well without theory to guide it	Action can respond sensitively to change
Theory produces pure knowledge	Situated action produces practice wisdom
Theory produces maps that the novice can safely rely upon	Situated action encourages novices to think on their feet
Activity is concentrated away from the field	Activity is focused on the field itself
Theory relies on contemplative distance from action	Situated action relies on embodied presence within action

Many therapists, and practitioners in other walks of life, will recognise 'what we are talking about', though they may never have given it a name. The reality it points to, which many share from their own practice, matters supremely – it is the wisdom derived from walking on the ground.

Naturally, rational systems have their place – in certain, limited settings they are the most effective form of operation. Without them the trains could not run on time, rockets go to a precise location in outer space, the light bulb turn on when we throw the switch. We would not wish our brain surgeon to be radically situated and working on intuition. Still it is true that not everything in reality is organised in this way. There is another territory that cannot be fully captured by the mind working alone – it is too wild, not at all reassuring, but exciting and interesting, and takes us 'out of our mind' and affects our heart.

In recent years we have seen the ever growing dominance of the *Diagnostic and Statistical Manual of Mental Disorders* (DSM), with insurance and drug companies driving an expanding number of diagnosable and categorisable mental health conditions. Publicly funded counselling interventions have been moving towards the shorter-term contract with an easily manualised set of interventions for the practitioner to work from. These are, after all, easier to research and cheaper to fund. A dangerous belief – that the rational capacity for abstract conceptualisation, orderly structure, reductive analysis, quantitative measurement and mechanical technique, will enable us to sort out another human being in distress and suffering – has taken hold. Therapy too is to be fully rationalised and turned into a science. The problem is – it does not work well when you try it out. It can produce very poor, and sometimes harmful, therapy. It leaves something out which really matters in the face-to-face meeting that is both the frame and engine of effective therapy. Living is meeting, so said Martin Buber (1923). Real therapy is meeting, geared toward healing.

If we are not careful, the patient, the diagnosis and the treatment become all too quickly mechanised – delivered by an increasingly mechanistic practitioner. But we are not machines – a suffering human being needs care, empathic attunement and compassionate responsiveness from a warm, present, engaged other – who in turn has suffered in trying to live fully in this world – if they are to find a space in which they can begin to take in transformational healing. If we simply throw a book full of abstract knowledge at a patient, why be there at all?

Nietzsche witheringly said of the rational vision abstracted out of life: 'It is about as useful as knowing the chemical composition of water would be to a drowning man'. When learning to swim in emotional, embodied real world situations, as Blaise Pascal said 'the heart has its reasons of which reason knows nothing' (1660, Section IV *Of the Means of Belief,* 242).

Therapy deals in what human beings existentially and practically face in living. Therapy must face this unknown in the very way it helps people face it.

SNAPSHOTS FROM REAL LIFE

Here are six snapshots from real life that convey different facets of practice wisdom. The first story is an account of my very first therapy session with a real client when I was in training – the last is a famous account of the trials of acting. The other four stories have been circulating for a long time.

Snapshot 1: The First Time is Always Scary
Having just completed a three-year under-graduate degree in psychology and counselling, I was armed to the gills with ideas, theories and knowledge about counselling and how it worked. The course had been excellent and had encouraged us, through reflective practice work, role play, group experiential work and teaching, to try and place ourselves in experience-near situations. In other words we practised on each other, taking turns being counsellor and client, giving one another feedback on our presence, body language, interventions and style. I remember being very eager to get 'out there' and really begin proper work with a real client.

In the first semester of my post-graduate clinical training I had finally managed to secure a training placement with an organisation that worked with people who were living with HIV/AIDS. My first assessment appointment was scheduled for a wet Tuesday evening in the West End of London with a young man we will call Neil, recently diagnosed HIV positive. For me, the build-up to this moment, the years of preparation, had left me feeling fairly sure that I knew what it would feel like to sit in a room with a real person with real problems and work with them therapeutically. After all I had practised it dozens of times. And read accounts of it in many books. And I had, briefly, been in therapy myself some years before. All of these things gave me a 'feel' for what therapy terrain would be like.

What I hadn't bargained on, however, was how I might change when the big moment came. My body, my senses and my mind started to react very strongly in the hour or so leading up to the first session. The wild horses were let loose: I was nervous. I suddenly doubted the things I had been taught. They seemed too simplistic and easy. Too clear-cut. My mouth was dry and during the walk down the stairs to fetch my client from the waiting room I would have given almost anything to be somewhere – anywhere – else. I felt like a fraud and I was scared I was about to be revealed as an absolute beginner who knew next to nothing. When Neil walked into the room for the first meeting I really could not say who was more terrified: me or him. It is hard to remember now but I suspect that Neil's experience did not figure too heavily on my radar screen during that first session. I was too busy trying to focus on whether I was sitting right, asking the right questions, and trying to remember the rules on empathy, challenging, open questioning and the like.

Eventually, after what seemed like an age, it ended. We agreed to meet the following week. At the start of session two Neil asked me if he could ask some questions. 'Of course,' I replied. His two questions were the two most devastating I have ever been asked in a therapy session: how old are you, and what are your qualifications? To be fair they were perfectly reasonable questions. He had obviously gone home feeling unnerved; am I in the hands of some young amateur? Is this going to be useful…or even safe? He had clearly been thinking about this throughout the week and plucked up the courage to ask me. I was 30 and that had been my very first session. What was there to say? I felt caught out and deeply exposed. If memory serves me correctly I think I took the classic therapeutic tack when cornered of wondering why he had asked me those questions. I don't recall much of the rest of the session.

Afterwards I felt flattened and was sure I had made a massive mistake in trying to become a therapist. It was clear that I was so transparent that my inexperience and nervousness was flashing like a warning light. The next week, session three, approached and I was sure in my mind that Neil was never coming back, having had a near escape from being mentally damaged by this eager newcomer. Surprisingly, he did return and we went on to do some reasonable work together.

In many years of practice since, and in thousands of other sessions, no one else has ever asked me those two questions in that way again.

What was the knowledge which I lacked when facing my first client? Why had all my academic study over years not prepared me for this moment? I was well versed in theories and techniques, and even had experience-near rehearsal in therapy role plays. Yet in the event of 'meeting the real thing', I suddenly felt completely at the mercy of powerful forces that undid my preparation.

What was there about this moment that was so challenging? Why was practising therapy with a real human being so different, and unique, such that no conceivable prior learning could wholly ready anyone for it? Even in training which is near to the reality, the consequences of our action are muted. When suddenly confronted by the reality of the mystery of another human being, the consequences bite. What enables us to both risk and weigh up such cost of action?

Snapshot 2: Improvising a Way Out of Trouble

In 1959, Johnny Weissmuller (the actor who played Tarzan) was in Cuba to play in a pro-celebrity golf match. At the time Fidel Castro's communist rebels were fighting Batista's soldiers for control of the country. Thus, his car contained not only a group of friends, but a number of bodyguards. On their way to the golf links the car was suddenly surrounded by a gang of armed guerrillas, who promptly disarmed Weissmuller's protectors, and pointed their guns at him and his party.

What would Tarzan do when faced with such danger? Weissmuller gallantly got out of the car. Rising to his full height, he beat his fists on his chest, and let out Tarzan's famous yodel. At first the guerrillas were in total shock, but then recognised the jungle hero from his movies. 'Tarzan! Tarzan!' they cried. 'Bienvenido! Welcome to Cuba!'

What was about to become a kidnapping, or worse, suddenly turned into an autograph session, following which 'Tarzan' and company were triumphantly escorted to the golf links.

What enabled Johnny Weissmuller to think so quickly in the face of the sudden physical danger looming over him and his friends? To come up with an instant and simple way to diffuse the tension and win the armed men over to his side was crucial to survival, and without any time to ruminate on what he should do, he 'just did it'.

To find himself in dire emergency was something Weissmuller could never have anticipated when he set out for what seemed an enjoyable and undemanding interlude; and, probably, if he had been granted foresight, and the time to think about the most appropriate response beforehand, it is unlikely he would have produced something so risky and creative, and yet perfectly attuned to the situation as it developed. The 'fit' between the problem posed by the situation and the solution in the 'heat of the moment' was profound. We call this 'hitting the target', or simply 'that was spot on', but just how extraordinary it is gets taken for granted.

We are able to knit together the most viable inner resource with the specific demands of the outer world, and do this knitting together spontaneously. What is this ability to think on our feet, and improvise, in order to be appropriate to the moment?

Snapshot 3: Small Details Can Make All the Difference

During the opening lap of the 1950 Monaco Grand Prix, Juan Manuel Fangio, an Argentinean racing driver, was approaching a particularly dangerous bend for the second time when he suddenly became aware that something was wrong. The faces of the spectators, which he usually saw as a whitish blur as he drove down the straight, were all turned away from him.

'If they are not looking at me', Fangio instantly realised, 'they must be looking at something more interesting around the corner.' He braked hard.

As he carefully rounded the bend, he saw that his split-second assessment of the situation had been accurate. The road was blocked by a pile-up of most of the other cars in the race. Fangio, who was nicknamed 'El Chueco' ('knock-kneed') or 'El Maestro', had saved his life.

What was unusual about the kind of attention Juan Manuel Fangio used to save his car and his life? What is this ability to be diffusely yet acutely aware of the world all around us, so that we can pick up even very small alterations in it, and adjust our ongoing action accordingly?

We are able to change course if the circumstances change. What is this ability of 'situational awareness' that allows activity to remain so sensitive to its surroundings that it can revise itself as it goes along?

 Snapshot 4: Turning Disaster into Triumph

While leading his men ashore at Pevensey in Sussex during the conquest of England in 1066, William inauspiciously stumbled and fell. Immediately his deeply suspicious and horrified men cursed the bad omen. However, William rose with a handful of soil.

'By the splendour of God, I have taken possession of my realm,' he cried. 'The earth of England is in my two hands!'

Passionate cheering spread throughout the ranks and the invasion was back on track.

William the Conqueror faced disaster of a different kind when, upon first treading on English soil, he tripped and fell. This might have been regarded as almost a judgement of God, declaring William's unsuitability for kingship over the land he was about to invade. As with Johnny Weissmuller, he had to spontaneously improvise some response in the moment which turned a potentially catastrophic situation to his resounding advantage. He had to not only think on his feet (or in this instance, flat on his face), but also think outside the box, reversing a king's humiliation through hitting the dirt into a king's befriending of the soil he will rule over.

There was no time for William to think out, nor give, a lengthy peroration designed to explain away, or justify, his fall. Its dark foreboding lay heavy on him and his men, like a shadow that comes from nowhere to blot out the sun. But by just one apposite 'word', everyone was so struck that the situation was turned upside down. The shadow was banished to reveal the sun shining brighter than before.

What is this capacity to be spontaneous, and improvise in a manner that is not only appropriate to a situation, but actually boldly influences and shifts the total configuration there, creating 'a whole new ball game' out of the downhill direction in which the old situation had been going?

 Snapshot 5: The Shock of the Real

Wilfred Owen, the English poet, set out for France on 30 December 1916. Nothing in his military training, and nothing in his fertile imagination, could have prepared him for what lay ahead in the trenches. He later described this as his 'first encounter with the reality of war'.

After joining the 2nd Manchesters on the Somme during January 1917, he wrote home to his mother: 'I can see no excuse for deceiving you about these last four days. I have suffered seventh hell…we had a march of nearly three miles over shelled road, then nearly three along a flooded trench. After that we came to where the trenches had been blown flat out and had to go over the top. It was of course dark, too dark and the ground was not mud, not sloppy mud, but an octopus of sucking clay, three, four and five feet deep, relieved only by craters of water…'.

Until he found himself in the situation of war, Owen could never have hoped to understand how it would affect him, physically, emotionally, psychologically, spiritually. Much of the poetry he wrote during World War I tried to convey the sense of the real horror to a patriotic and fervent public at home who still delighted in stories of glory and honour. In the final stanza of his poem 'Dulce et Decorum Est' he wrote:

> If in some smothering dreams you too could pace
> Behind the wagon that we flung him in,
> And watch the white eyes writhing in his face,
> His hanging face, like a devil's sick with sin;
> If you could hear, at every jolt, the blood
> Come gargling from the froth-corrupted lungs,
> Obscene as cancer, bitter as the cud
> Of vile, incurable sores on innocent tongues,
> My friend, you would not tell with such high zest
> To children, ardent for some desperate glory,
> The old Lie: Dulce et Decorum Est
> Pro Patria Mori.

(From *Poems with an introduction by Siegfried Sassoon*, 1920, p.11)

The Latin phrase 'dulce et decorum est pro patria mori' ('it is sweet and right to die for your country') came to seem like an obscene lie to Owen after even a limited exposure to the real 'theatre of war'.

Wilfred Owen's experience is testified to by many who have been in war. The consequences of the actions we perform, and the actions performed by others, are suddenly ultimate. War is the 'limit situation' (Marcel 1952) that reveals why everything dramatically changes when we must commit to action in the actual setting; action has a cost, for oneself and for others, and that cost can be hard to pay.

However empathically we read Owen's poem, we cannot pace behind the wagon where that young soldier is battling for his life. We try to imagine its awfulness but part of the horror lies in knowing that we are touching but a pale fragment of the reality. Owen's point is that experience is different; it changes us profoundly, it leaves its marks on us, we will never be the same again.

Why did Owen speak of the 'shock of the real' to describe what it was like when he first faced war? He is not merely making the point that no training can prepare a soldier for the reality of war; he is, much more basically, trying to tell a complacent populace that such reality is betrayed by idealised accounts of it that totally falsify its ground-level truth. Idealising any reality we must face on the ground betrays the truth both of what it is like, and what it is like for us to have to meet it face to face.

We have to stand up to many kinds of cutting edge in all our experience of the terrain, without running away or going under. What enables us to get stuck in, see it through, emerge out the other side, strengthened, and wiser?

 Snapshot 6: But I Don't Know How I Did It!
Laurence Olivier once tried something in his portrayal of Shakespeare's *Othello* that by general consensus was, if not wrong-headed, then at the very least odd. Though Shakespeare calls Othello a 'Moor', meaning an Arab from North Africa, specifically Morocco, Olivier decided to represent him on stage as a Jamaican. Movement, gesture, facial expression, accent, were all carefully nuanced to be as authentically West Indian as a white man disguised in black paint could achieve. Though his sheer skill in pulling off this feat of mimicry was admired, some who saw the play felt the whole enterprise was doomed from the start. At a deeper level, this imposture just did not work, however technically adroit. Others took it differently. One reviewer called

the performance poetic, primal, athletic, likening Olivier on stage to a great prowling panther.

Olivier must have felt this ambiguity in what he was doing in his bones, for it is said he used to suffer terrible nerves both before he went on, and during the play. But one night, Olivier shed his obsession with technical perfection, which caused some people to see him as slightly over the top and something of a ham actor, and came up with what everyone who witnessed it regarded as the greatest acting performance he had ever given. Indeed, some critics rated this performance among the greatest of all time. When an actor gets inside a character confined to the page and makes him live as if he were a real human being, expressing his inner life outwardly, and communicating this to the audience, something magical occurs. In ordinary parlance we hardly do justice to such events by saying 'it all came together'.

Olivier was a creature of ritual. He would always formally acknowledge the audience's applause with a stately bow. On this night, he bowed only perfunctorily to the rapturous clapping and shouts drowning the National Theatre stage, and then abruptly disappeared into his dressing room, locking the door behind him. His two female co-stars, Maggie Smith and Joyce Redman, were concerned by this very odd reaction, and even felt some guilt, because they had played a trick on 'Larry' earlier this night. Another ritual that he always followed was to drink a glass of champagne, left awaiting him in the dressing room fridge, in the interval between acts. But the two women had snuck in ahead of him, and drank all the bubbly. They were worried that Olivier had taken severe umbrage at their prank.

They approached his dressing room door tentatively, and knocked softly. 'Larry, why are you upset?' Olivier shouted out at them, 'Go away.' They called in to him, 'Your performance tonight was simply superb, your best ever. We want to congratulate you. Please come out.' Then, getting no word from within, they added: 'We're sorry we drank your champagne.' There was an ominous silence. Then the dressing room door opened a crack. 'Why are you so upset?' the women pleaded with Olivier.

The door was flung wide open, and with consternation on his face and exasperation filling his body, Olivier threw his arms in the air, and revealed why he had stormed off and locked himself away. 'I know it was my greatest ever acting performance,' he told them, 'but I am upset because I have no idea how I did it!'

Why was Laurence Olivier so upset that he had given his greatest ever acting performance without knowing how he did it? Olivier was famous for being one of the most thoroughly rehearsed actors ever: his performances were marked by meticulous and detailed prior choreographing of every move, expression, inflection. He hated to leave anything to chance. But he was also capable of letting the here-and-now relationship with the

audience, so potent in the theatre, move him such that he could infuse the manoeuvres he had rehearsed in isolation with an inspiration that lifted them onto a different level.

What enables us to make what is very familiar to us new and fresh each time we return to it, rather than settling into boring habit?

Obviously, improvising in the heat of the moment, and the freedom to be creative, is not possible if the person 'sticks to the script'. But sticking to the script seems to guarantee a consistency in performance, even if this becomes more and more robotic and tedious, less and less moving and exciting. Olivier knew that perfectly well. But he was upset because he did not trust that this knowing what to do that wells up intuitively as we proceed, without our knowing how it is done, would return and be reliably available whenever he needed it. This intuitive support to action in the real world seemed too elusive, and possibly fickle. To count on it would be foolish, like diving into deep waters not sure whether we can swim.

So at the outset we must draw some distinctions between the models-led way and the situated-action way.

Differences between the models-led way and the situated-action way	
Models-Led Way	**Situated-Action Way**
Is top down – one way	Is bottom up – two way
Is about instructing and controlling the world	Is about dialoguing and being with the world
Relies on technical skill	Relies on craftsmanship know how
Involves repeatable and mechanical action	Has exploratory action
Sees errors and failures as serious problems	Understands they are the only way to learn
Gold standard: the same every time	Gold standard: subtly different every time

NOT ANTI MODELS, ANTI MODELS-LED

Therapy models are after-the-fact reconstructions of therapeutic practice in the field. This means they arose as 'reflection on practice'. They emerged out of first-person accounts of discovery, made by many travellers, and their collective weight helps promote, encourage and facilitate new travellers in their discovery process. They do not provide perfect maps – that would be to abuse their whole point and ethos – but can offer signposts for helping us in our own walking. They are maps constructed by therapy pioneers 'after' their personal walk. Though we might wish to take this account of the 'way someone else walked' as a hard-and-fast instruction for our walking the same terrain, can the previously established route ever really be walked again? Given that the real world constantly changes it follows that whenever we return to it, we will find it is more or less different. No two clients are alike. Even single clients alter session to session, moment to moment. As practitioners we are constantly changing and evolving ourselves. Abstract models claim fixed knowledge of a predictably static and clear-cut world, but knowledge of an unpredictably changing and ambiguous world has to be more open and fluid as we have already established. 'A' map can never be the one and only map.

Accepting that the reported and abstracted experiences of others can only ever function as 'looser guidance' rather than definitive instruction opens up the necessity of reaching our own hard-won 'practice wisdom'. Our walk through the terrain can never be their walk. The 'rough guide full of travellers' tales' is a teaching of wisdom, and remains enigmatic, not fully spelt out. A degree of clarity and structure can crystallise out of reflection on action in the field and offer some guidelines but it does not pretend the landmark features on a map are any sort of hard-and-fast 'failsafe' of what to do when travelling in the real world. Such humble models realise that it requires 'situated drivers' to operate effectively on the ground.

The arrogant models, by contrast, foolishly and blindly believe that their retrospective account of walking through the terrain is to be treated not simply as a beacon of light to help us on rough ground but as unquestionable prescription, to be followed obediently and exactly by those who come next. They are a trap for the wary and nervous walker, new to the territory, desperate for some certainty and guidance. Gabriel Marcel, the French existential philosopher, expressed the essence of this relationship between knowledge and being: 'knowledge is contingent on a participation in being for which no epistemology can account... knowledge is within being, enfolded by it' (1952, p.84). Most models-led thinking fails to recognise this, indeed would mock the very idea of this being so; nevertheless it is fundamentally correct and many writers, thinkers and practitioners have acknowledged it.

To summarise the argument so far:

- The driving force of models-led practice, both philosophically and psychologically, is **expectation**.

- The driving force of situated action, both philosophically and psychologically, is **discovery**.

- In models-led practice, expectation operates through a monologue imposed on the world. In situated action, discovery operates through dialogue negotiated with the world.

THE MAP CANNOT ADEQUATELY REPRESENT THE TERRAIN

The map easily becomes too abstract. Abstract thought shelters from the real by preferring generality, but reality never presents itself to us in meeting it on the ground as just the 'particular instance' of some generic rule. You don't meet on the ground the general-category cat, you meet a succession of particular cats, each unique. Plato and Aristotle used this example of 'catness' to explore their different philosophical approaches – with Plato favouring abstract conceptualising about cats and Aristotle privileging the actual experience of meeting with a particular cat (Howard 2000, p.41). Abstractionism tends to gloss over that the different cats have their own flesh and blood, their unique matter, personality and spirit which mean any encounter with them is never mechanistic or predictable.

It is all too easy to claim as part of your theoretical orientation that you have warmth and unconditional positive regard for all your clients but on the ground you always meet with a very particular human being, replete with all their quirks, foibles, distressing habits, defensive manoeuvres and unexpected responses. You must meet with, work with, dialogue with, love with – him or her.

To walk this in reality is much harder than to simply talk it. To really immerse ourselves in the emotional, psychological and energetic world of another living person is far more dynamic, terrifying, uplifting and moving than any written account (either before or after the fact) can ever capture. The map will always be drier, flatter, safer and cleaner than the contoured real world which is juicy, dirty, wet and dangerous. But we know that real food is tastier than the menu, climbing the mountain more satisfying than the outline in the guidebook and the breathing, moving, responding body touches you in ways a picture never can. It is also true, naturally, that the food can poison you; the menu cannot. During the climb you can fall; in the guidebook you cannot. The picture will not break your heart but the lover most certainly can.

The map feels safer, easier to control – and many retreat there to live something akin to a half-life. The terrain can potentially wound and destroy you but is drenched in colour, awareness, energy and change. It requires us to risk something, to be open to profound reshaping of who we are. Intellectualisation and defensive thought try to cut corners and eventually they deny reality, tending to 'iron out' the ground's ambiguous patterns, so they appear more sensible and coherent than they really are. They promise to spare us from the lows whilst depriving us of the highs. The worst of this kind of thought pretends reality is like a crossword puzzle, presenting a well-defined problem that has an equally well-defined solution. This offers us the tempting and seductive illusion of safety. This may make us *feel* better for a time – but actually leaves us under-prepared and vulnerable when travelling on the ground. It is a form of shutting one's eyes and hoping for the best. No matter how far we retreat into our cognitive mind we cannot remain there permanently unless we mean to avoid human relational contact altogether. For any practising therapist to do this is terrifying and wholly unacceptable.

Reality tests and pushes us, but moves us profoundly. This is why we must 'try it out' and 'go through it' for ourselves. The mystery, the pain and the joy of life is in the colourful, maddening, extraordinary details on the ground; but all this beautiful texture and depth, richness and quality, disappears in the too sweeping thought which prefers theorising because it does not want to deal with practical and existential variety. The discipline of reflective practice thinking is to never cut the tie to experience, since this is what immerses us in the terrain's humanity. To understand a terrain, we must be affected by it, involved, interested.

Given its experiential and enactive dimensions, situated functioning is easier to teach to students in the field, or on the job, than to describe to a reader on the page. For example, the way in which several strands come together in action that is relevant to its setting is hard to state exactly. We say, 'I finally got my act together', and everyone knows what we mean, but this expression is a shorthand that suffices for a deeply complex process.

Any given therapy model – that of Freud, Jung, Adler, Rogers, Perls, Ellis, Beck, Fairbairn, Kohut, *et al.* – is no more or no less than a record of the route *someone* took in their walk through the terrain of therapising.

After their walk, they reflected on what got them through, what the helps and hindrances were, and tried to convey this by articulating it as a map and a plan. Some therapists did convey the lessons they learned in the field, and the organic ideas these sparked, in the thinking and language of reflective practice. Most founding fathers and mothers, unfortunately, developed their practitioner knowledge of the field into full-blown models with sets of precise directions and theoretical structures for others to follow. Some therapeutic practice by orthodox Freudians (especially after his death) typifies the very worst of what happens when the pure (and usually misunderstood) instructions of the founder are carved in stone. Whether in politics, religion or therapy practice what follows is often damaging or dangerous. The theorist is reified as a grand visionary, who can save their future followers from having to wrestle with reality themselves or develop their own practical wisdom. And, sadly, many are only too happy to give away their power, their intelligence and their agency to someone else who promises a shortcut, quick-fix, easy way to mastery.

Therefore, this book is saying to the situated practitioner: 'Own the special quality of what you know by realising how extraordinary it is that you can know this. You are engaged in a practising that has its own existential and practical wisdom, its own poetic craft, and its own service of something ultimately valuable, all linked in an unbreakable fabric of interlacing threads'.

This being so, there is such a person as a wise healer, and there is such a thing as the wisdom of healing.

This wisdom grows over time, inside us, in the well – the portable, personal system of practical wisdom that will assist and guide us whilst in the terrain of working with clients. In reality we are our own well – it is our brain, our memory, our heart, spirit, body, energy, confidence and personality which holds this incredible resource for us, often at a level below everyday consciousness, in the implicit mind, in body memory. It is this location (outside of ordinary conscious awareness) which makes us doubt that the bucket will come up full this time when we move inside the territory. This is the source of all performance anxiety – in therapy, in business, in acting.

Over many years of discussing, teaching, living and working with this set of lived phenomena I have outlined a very useful metaphor for how the well fills up: a number of streams of living water that flow into the well and replenish its supply – the streams fill the bucket with that intangible something which appears when we enter the real-world territory of practice. I have encouraged students, clients, colleagues and myself to reflect on these streams, to discuss and to journal around them, to act them out, draw them and feel them – to practise them as frequently as possible so that we can recognise and understand their existence within the self. Eventually we can rely on and be supported by them in each new return to the living, breathing territory of client work. The next section sets out 34 streams that flow into the well.

Part 2

THE STREAMS OF PRACTICE WISDOM

Continually developing and enhancing these streams within oneself must be paramount during our training (and in our continuing life as a practitioner) if we are to work, and act, on the ground intelligently and sensitively. In short, these streams are the very things that not only make situated action possible, but also, when they are learned and developed to their maximum, they allow practice wisdom to operate extremely well.

I call them the streams of situated action as they form the content that flows into the well of practical wisdom growing inside each therapy practitioner as they travel from apprenticeship to mastery. Water is the best metaphor to use here as the content is always fluid, changing, unpredictable and energised. If rigid models-led practice is best symbolised by ice (water that is frozen, static, measureable and predictable); situated action is best symbolised by living, moving water that responds, changes and flows over time – it never stays the same. It follows therefore that the underpinning philosophies of models-led versus situated action are fundamentally different: to really inhabit what follows it is important to take a moment to ponder on the different philosophical platforms upon which the two approaches sit.

Differences between models-led philosophy and situated-action philosophy	
Models-Led Philosophy	**Situated-Action Philosophy**
Overviews the world in advance	Finds out through exploration
Plans ahead	Improvises
Once in the field is fixed and formulaic	In the field is flexible and responsive
Separates idea and action	Brings ideas and actions together
Watches from a distance to maximise control	Participates via immersion and dialogue
Thinks in the abstract	Thinks in the concrete
Uses conscious, rational, formulated processes	Uses unconscious, intuitive, tacit processes
Is about recipes	Is about adventure
Seeks cast-iron guarantees	Accepts risk and transformation

This particular set of 34 streams has emerged for me (and the many colleagues, students and clients I have worked with over the past two decades); I am in no way claiming that these are the only streams (or indeed the most important ones at all). To do so would be contrary to the spirit of situated action and would hinder therapists rather than assist them. They merely represent the experiential phenomena I have found best supported me in the ongoing building of practice wisdom and its associated stances, attitudes and counselling skills.

None of the streams have been 'invented' or 'discovered' anew by me or anyone else – as such they do not represent an alternative therapeutic model or refinement of existing models. Rather they have grown out of my increasing self-awareness and experience as a living, experiencing human being and as a practising counselling psychologist, teacher, researcher and supervisor. Every one of them has been noted and explored in some way by previous writers, theorists and practitioners – in the world of psychotherapy and elsewhere – but I do feel that outlining them together in this way does constitute something new and worthwhile.

CHAPTER 1
HOVERING ON THE EDGE

- The Leap of Faith
- Discovery
- The Journey
- Adventure

One of the main things blocking people from becoming situated is what happens when they stand on the threshold of new and potentially frightening experience. It is precisely then that our nerves may be at their most intense, our body's autonomic nervous system is telling us to fight, run or freeze, rather than perform, adrenaline is surging through us, and our mind will often start to run a very familiar script. 'This is scary, I don't really know what I am doing here, it could go wrong, what if people laugh, or think less of me, what might the consequences be, it's going to be too hard, I've forgotten what I thought up earlier, what if I'm not as good as last time.'

This point of hovering prior to take-off is often when the lazy, frightened, tired, scared, doubtful, part of us is screaming at its loudest. Just turn around, go home, why do I put myself through this, let somebody else deal with it.

As I have mentioned, in my own practice, where I have wrestled with this problem, I have found it helpful to remember that there is a personal 'well' of situated knowing inside which can come out when needed. Your bucket is empty yet shortly a surging of water is going to be necessary. There is a restless crowd (or eager client) in front of you whose thirst you must quench from a seemingly empty vessel, trusting that by stepping into the intersubjective space of the field something will happen. You must trust that the flow will occur. Something inside of you, your implicit mind, will start to respond. Just at the moment you step off the edge, on stage, onto the playing field, in front of the audience, open the door to let your client into the session, there is nothing solid under your feet, only potential. It is then we screw our courage to the sticking place, and step forward regardless.

This is the key to it all. Just before the step the well can seem relatively dry and empty; across the threshold the water starts pouring. Imagine looking at the pack containing a parachute whilst still sitting in the plane. It doesn't look like a parachute right now and there is a possibility, however tiny, that it may not open and you will fall to your death. But you cannot see the open chute while you are still in the plane. You are required to leap out into mid-air first before it can open and do its job. This is the paradox – the flow of the implicit mind that shows up in the field cannot show up outside of the field for it only lies dormant there. Facsimiles of it do exist there but they are illusions masquerading as the real thing. In truth you will only experience memories, projections, plans and rehearsals, never the real deal. The rehearsal can never be the performance – training can never be war.

After the leap is taken something profound can happen; you react to the field and it responds to you, a different energy begins to grow in the co-created space between you – and the well really starts to pump. It is then we can have moments of engaged flow and creative inspiration where afterwards we shake our heads in wonder and say, 'Where on earth did that come from?'

Just as leaping from a height into mid-air seems counter logical if we want to be safe, so does the step beyond the threshold into the unknown territory ahead. And yet something inside frees up when we are willing to move. Waiting and endlessly wishing for something to come and save us from this state of vacuity, anxiety and doubt, rarely works. We have to start moving before things begin shifting and bending in reply to our call.

The key to this process is to recognise that in moving into intersubjective space we leave behind the purely subjective self, however temporarily, as we move into dialogue, relationship and communion. Most honest therapists will tell you that some days, just before a session, they may be full of their own woes, flat, tired, even in pain, and wondering how they will manage today to be a calm, listening, empathic presence for their client. Maybe today my 'shadow' feels heavier than my client's, maybe they should be listening to me. Many times I have experienced that heavy sense of self fall away, like a shed skin, as I move into the new space with the client. For that hour I get a rest from myself, break free of the bonds that are my own confined self, and connect to something larger outside of me.

This helps liberate us from the chains of the most limiting aspects of the subjective self, as we are propelled into intersubjective space. This is the true engine at the heart of the situated process. It is also true, however, that not all leaps of faith need massive jumps. Sometimes only a small step is needed to begin engrossing ourselves in the phenomenon before us.

In this chapter, *'Hovering on the Edge'*, I introduce the first four streams that need to develop near the start of our journey. They are particularly useful to introduce to those currently training to be counsellors, psychotherapists, psychologists or helpers. In truth they apply to anyone in the apprentice state of mind; they are about standing on the starting line and the anticipation of what is to come – whether you are a footballer, a dentist, a parent or a dancer. You cannot reach mastery – or any genuine pool of practical wisdom – without travelling through this stage at first.

STREAM 1: THE LEAP OF FAITH

> Concerning all acts of initiative and creation there is one elementary truth – that the moment one definitely commits oneself, then providence moves too. All sorts of things occur to help one that would never otherwise have occurred and which no man could have dreamed would have come their way.
>
> Johannes Wolfgang Von Goethe

We all have inside of us a world of intellectual thought (which we like to believe is objective) and a subjective world of emotion. It is through these cognitive and psychological lenses that we view, hear and experience the world. We have lived within this internal space our whole lives, we are used to it, and although the internal voice in our head may sometimes be unkind or cruel to the self – broadly this space is a security blanket, a place we can retire to when the external world gets to be too much. Some people are able to convince themselves that everything they think and feel within this space is broadly right. The ego says my way is the better way. This individual security blanket can be hard to let go of. In psychology we call this the *intrapsychic* space. This internal self constantly has to dialogue with, relate to, defend against, co-operate with other people: in *interpersonal* space.

The 'self-system' (Sullivan 1953)

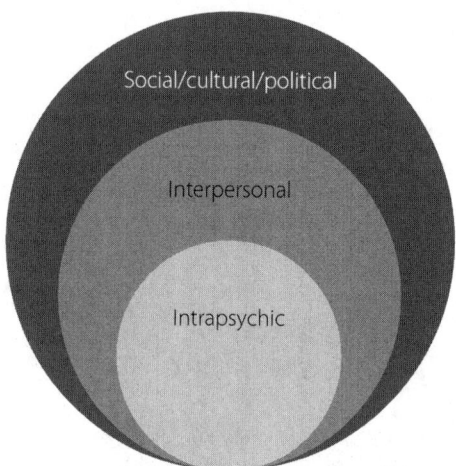

How the personality develops

Both of these, in turn, are affected by the socio-cultural, political and economic space which surrounds them. Harry Stack Sullivan (1953), the Interpersonal Psychoanalyst, visualised this as the *self-system*.

Encounters with others – first in being parented, building friendships, working together, falling out, falling in love, having our own children – all involve temporarily leaving the inner familiar world we know and trying to connect to an outside world that is not us. We meet the unknown when we step into the intersubjective realm, and this is the point where we are apt to freeze and become paralysed. That step crosses a strangely intimidating threshold and we can feel like the proverbial non-swimmer about to be thrown into deep water where it is 'sink or swim'. Even if the non-swimmer is reassuringly told by those who have learned to swim that the water will uphold them, they still must risk this, and try it out for themselves. If the non-swimmer will not venture this initial danger, then they can get stuck in a vicious circle from which it is not possible to break out.

The Streams in the Consulting Room

LEAP OF FAITH

Merely entering the therapy room is a leap of faith for most clients – many are scared, unsure, worry about being judged, feel hopeless or lost when they arrive.

No matter whether we have seen dozens or hundreds of clients as therapists we must never forget that the person walking into our room today is likely to be in a place of some crisis, possibly suffering more psychologically than ever before.

Each new client – and each new session – requires us as practitioners to take the leap. Will I get it right today? Can I ever really understand this person? Am I feeling too overwhelmed, sad or lost in my life to be truly present for them right now?

The truth is, only if I plunge into the water will I find that it can uphold me. No one else can do that for me, or tell me it is so. I must take the plunge, and uncover that truth about my relationship to the water only from within it. If I refuse submersion due to what 'might' happen when I jump in, and will only entertain jumping in if I can be given iron-clad reassurances and protections in regard to what I imagine as the worst, then I will have excused myself from ever trying the water. This becomes a self-fulfilling prophecy. The more the bird sitting on a perch high up in the air refuses to trust the air by flapping his wings in flight, so the more those wings atrophy, and if he ever did tentatively flap them, he would probably fall from his perch. The bird has to flap his wings and lean on the air to find out that air will support wings, and what wings can and cannot do in regard to air. This is how confidence is built.

Reflection Point

LEAP OF FAITH

- *How have you felt when you have been on the point of a huge decision or something scary and new?*
- *What helped you decide to make the jump?*
- *What were the reasons you may have held back?*
- *How might clients be feeling when they take the leap of faith to come to a first session?*

Existential writers have also referred to the existential 'Leap of Faith'. Kierkegaard (1985 [1843]) offers a powerful image of the leap when he attempts to describe true faith, trying to overcome the limits of reason and rejecting the requirement that everything be smooth or easy to obtain. Nietzsche (1969 [1891]) in *Thus Spake Zarathustra* sees man as walking on a 'rope over an abyss', upon which we must learn to balance, dance and leap if we are ever to change. He felt that ultimately all philosophical thought was based on some kind of leap of faith. This is why it is the first in our set of streams – it provides a platform on which all the others can rest. One of the Reflective Practice students put it like this:

Student Excerpt
After reading the streams this year, the Leap of Faith has definitely had the biggest influence on me – especially concerning engaging with peer students who are not necessarily part of my close social circle. Instead of imagining what their hidden agendas might be, or what they might be thinking of me, I confront these thoughts. I know that distrusting my peers has deprived me of opportunities to contribute in class, to make new discoveries and even make a better connection with my fellow students. After reflecting on my experiences with the trust circle [an outdoor group exercise exploring trust, power and caretaking in an embodied way], I started challenging myself – making myself take the leap of faith instead of hiding behind my defensive wall of suspicions.

In essence this stream's advice is: don't wait for the universe to come to you or hide in fearfulness waiting for someone to rescue you. It won't. They won't. If you are brave enough to take that first vulnerable step, then something in the terrain starts to respond to you. This is the required 'leap of faith'.

Zen acknowledges the paradox: 'In the mind of the Beginner there are many possibilities, but in the mind of the expert there are few' (Zen, traditional). Later we will consider the situated knowing of the truly advanced practitioner that combines freshness and accomplishment, chaos and clarity, open-endedness and structure, in a sophisticated unity. But for now, it can be admitted that what Zen calls 'Beginner's Mind' has a kind of ignorance in starting out that proves oddly enabling. This is obvious not just in the well-known fact of 'beginner's luck', where beginners do extraordinary things because of not realising how impossible they are, but also in recognising that beginners come up with creative solutions to problems missed by more seasoned heads. The odd power of the

Beginner's Mind is something that, in a sense, should stay with us, as a foundation stone, even as we learn and improve our knowing and develop more skill.

> To be uncertain is uncomfortable, but to be certain is ridiculous.
>
> Chinese proverb

Beginner's Mind also has another attribute that is vital for the situated practitioner, and this is a willingness to admit to one's poverty, since this is what knowledge can enrich. For the most part we resist admitting to any such impoverishment, and insist we are already rich. In fact, most of our riches turn out to be, as far as the situated process is concerned, worthless. Some people carry around a huge mental clutter, made up of baseless opinions, ingrained prejudices and unexamined beliefs.

Not knowing means accepting the mystery of things. This allows them to be what they are, not what we think them to be, and to come forth according to their own nature, not be put in a cage of what we require them to be.

 The Key to the LEAP OF FAITH lies in the old Susan Jeffers idea – feel the fear and do it anyway! (Jeffers 2007)

STREAM 2: DISCOVERY

He who never made a mistake never made a discovery.

Samuel Smiles

Discovery stands in opposition to the models-led main mindset of expectation. It is the fluid running water that is unpredictable yet deeply creative versus the frozen water that is fully predictable yet impotent, barren, static. It implies the embracing of change, never arriving, rather than fear and resistance of the new: relishing the battle and playing, rather than running away from it.

Situated intelligence tunes in to 'what is happening', by accepting that its key significances can only emerge over time through dialogue which unpacks the situation. Too much 'knowledge in advance' rules out surprise and the happy accident – when things we plan don't work while accidents turn out to be wonderful. And, if we can know before being in and going through situations what their meaning or truth is, why bother to be there or try things out there? Why bother to 'live'?

From the moment we are born into this world we are thrown into a world of discovery. Everything is new: potentially hard to master but full of a fresh excitement that pulls us towards growth, development and eventual mastery of new skills. On our first day we can do very little for ourselves. We cannot walk, talk, reason or regulate our temperature, our appetites, our emotions or our bowels. We can cry, and we can gaze into our mother's face, we can root and we can suck. We need someone loving and present to do most things for us (if we are lucky). As we grow we gradually develop more of these capacities for ourselves: we move from *primary merger* with a mother figure towards an increasingly independent self via a process that Margaret Mahler (Mahler, Pine and Bergman 1973) called *individuation-separation*. As many psychologists and therapists have noted, this emergence of self from the cocoon of symbiosis is usually fraught with the issue of separation anxiety – for both the child and their parents. A central truth of the situated action-reflective practice approach is that moving into new, challenging and unknown territory is nearly always going to be accompanied by high levels of anxiety. When human beings experience overwhelming feelings of anxiety the autonomic nervous system responds to signals from the amygdala in the reptilian part of the human brain and goes into *fight, flight or freeze* mode. The body responds to these signals by releasing huge amounts of adrenaline and cortisol and we notice bodily signals: such as increased heart rate, sweating, blood flowing to the major muscle groups and away from the body's extremities and rising feelings of fear, dread, panic or terror accompanied by cognitive distortions about our sensations which lead to catastrophic misinterpretations of what the body is doing and what this means. For instance, panic disorder patients will commonly think they are going to faint, or are having a heart attack or 'going crazy' when their *fight–flight–freeze* system kicks into gear.

The Streams in the Consulting Room

DISCOVERY

Truly meeting every new client is a process of discovery – as is developing self-awareness and practice wisdom. We must be open to uncovering ever deeper layers of relational meeting in therapy, responding compassionately to even the darkest layers of human experiencing and discovering ways of staying fresh in the work even when we have heard the stories many times before.

How do you actively create a space of permission to allow clients to feel safe and trusting enough to go on this journey of discovery into their internal world with you?

In the past year what new things have you discovered about yourself as a practitioner?

In practice we tend to *run away* (avoid the anxiety-inducing experience, leave the scene when fear emerges, experience feelings of panic), *fight back* against the anxiety-inducing stimuli (by becoming angry, physically attacking, controlling or aggressive) or *withdraw* from it psychologically (by avoiding, repressing, disassociating, shutting down, using muscular tension or armouring). In the process of discovering newness we are likely to experience many occasions when this threat evaluation system comes alive. We must be able to experience this and still continue the journey of discovery. This is very hard – and without encouragement many adults will talk themselves out of trying new things. Thank goodness babies and toddlers are not like this or the human race would be in serious trouble. Human beings under the age of five can barely restrain themselves from gathering new information about the world around them. They are full of fascination and wonder for novelty and learning. They love to repeat experiences over and over – this is how the brain learns and at this age it is still in its most plastic form, billions of neurons looking to form networks based on the child's cognitive, spatial and emotional networks – or as Hebbian theory (Hebb 1949) in neuroscience puts it: 'neurons that fire together – wire together!'

Reflection Point

DISCOVERY

- *When you stand on the edge of something unknown, what feelings predominate for you – excitement, fear, lack of control, curiosity, self-doubt, aloneness, eagerness, impatience?*
- *Some people are so frightened by the process of discovery they build lives which avoid it, clinging to the familiar even if it hurts or constrains them.*
- *Others are addicted to intensity and novelty, rarely lingering in any field long enough to discover its true richness, depth and complexity.*
- *Where on this spectrum would you place yourself?*

Somewhere during our journey through childhood, adolescence and into adulthood many of us become blocked in this process – what once felt like a wholly natural and spontaneous thing – entering an excited mode of *discovery* – can shift towards a mode of *expectation*. As we grow older we tend to approach newness in one of three ways:

- seeking to control it by amassing knowledge, theory, systems or expertise

- feeling scared of it because we fear failure, or pain or loss, or doubt our own abilities or are crippled by worry at the thought of others judging or mocking us

- still feeling excited – watchful maybe, nervous perhaps, yet fundamentally still open to the newness and willing to take the walk.

The older we get the more likely we are to spend more time in the first and second states. School, work, even our families, teach us to be careful, risk-averse, sure of our ground before we start walking. Perhaps the most tragic aspect of the absence of discovery is that we miss so much of what is right in front of us. A student puts it like this:

> **Student Excerpt**
> I found out that there is so much more to things than we allow ourselves to see. We make assumptions about so much of what we see and just accept these as fact, without examination. I suppose this is for convenience, and for speed; spend too long looking and you don't get things done. And we find it useful to categorise, to put things into compartments that match things we have seen in the past. It's also about wanting to be in command, telling ourselves we know what we are dealing with, so we can handle it, but this closes us off to experiencing the true nature of what is there.

Therapists cannot afford to adopt the lazy way people pass through existence without really taking account of all that is there. Reality constantly surprises us because it is never really standing still. A static knowledge of the regular ticking over of reality may be useful for sending a rocket ship into space and getting it to Mars. But this cannot work in human terrain. Yet, it does not follow that the situated learner is without knowledge. It is just a different kind of knowledge.

This goes right to the heart of the paradox in situated functioning: on the one hand, the situated practitioner knows an immense amount about matters vital to the domain in which they are operating, but on the other hand, this 'familiarity' with their specific domain does not make them function like the rigid theoretician: a well-rehearsed robot. The violin player spends years acquiring technique so that, in the real performance, they can forget technique altogether, and concentrate on what really matters, which is the beauty of the music and how this is expressed for and communicated to the audience.

This is a way of saying that reality exceeds, like a huge cornucopia, any knowledge that is trying to be adequate to it. Reality is inexhaustible. Knowing is relative to reality, and thus we should resist the temptation to try to make reality relative to knowing.

 The Key to DISCOVERY is finding reserves of both humility and daring within you.

STREAM 3: THE JOURNEY

We don't receive wisdom: we must discover it for ourselves after a journey that no one can take for us or spare us.

Marcel Proust

Direct encounter with the situation would produce no learning *if experience and action were not the interactive bridges between the person and the world*. If we are experientially shut down our ability to learn from situations is horribly curtailed. One of the later streams explores the idea of Balance and this is crucial as we begin our journey. The previous stream, Discovery, requires a certain amount of wandering, getting lost, seeing what lies around that unexpected corner. However, for situatedness to function properly we humans do also seem to need an objective. This comes back to the notion of how best to use the map, the compass, the guidebook when in childlike exploratory mode so that it supports and enhances our full-of-wonder child rather than freezes them through an overload of fearful apprehension. Usually, at a deep human level, we need to feel we are moving forward, towards something, rather than being static or stuck. We know that time is constant, we age and we die and there is an imperative feeling to attain things; time is surely running out on us.

The reality of the paradoxical nature of human existence lies at the heart of the situated approach. In many spiritual teachings this notion is referred to as the 'divine paradox' – our experience of reality is dual, polarised: love and hate, light and dark, up and down, hot and cold, east and west, absolute and relative, concrete and abstract. We tend to language these as extremes, poles, either-ors. He loves me, he loves me not. The truth is that all these polarities exist on a spectrum. The child's mind may need to understand these as black and white, yes or no answers, what Melanie Klein (1975 [1946]) called 'splitting' or the 'paranoid-schizoid' position (more of which later). The mature mind accepts that everything mixes up elements of good and bad – nothing is perfect (what Klein cheerily calls 'the depressive position'). Learning to move up and down these spectra and not reside only at either pole is the work of a lifetime (maybe many lifetimes!) for both us and our clients.

Our awareness of life's journey is parallelled in our journey towards wise practice and expertise. When we begin a journey we tend to want to rush to the end ('are we there yet?'). We fantasise about the destination and what it will offer us in terms of status, completion, money, acceptance or boosted self-esteem. How often do we look back after an experience or a period of our lives and only then know that it was in the journey that the maximum pleasure and feeling was derived? Not in the reaching of the destination. This is also true of experience. And in developing as a practitioner our experiential journey never ends.

Student Excerpt

Often we focus on the point of arrival at our destination, omitting to savour the experiences along the way, not valuing the journey itself. Yet it is not the destination that matters, so much as the struggles and pleasures involved in getting there. For we never truly arrive at a destination, rather at a point where one journey ends and another begins, so it is important that we take the time to experience where we are, in the here-and-now, at this point of the journey, rather than striding ahead with our eyes fixed on the horizon. Because mortality is our ultimate fate, and it would be a shame to hasten towards that without having slowed down, lived authentically, found the courage to face the pain and disappointments in life and taken the time to experience its joys and wonders.

What matters to us on the journey can alter almost moment to moment, especially as a consequence of our action. Our action creatively changes the prevailing conditions, as well as sensitively responding to them: thus our action can tip the balance of the positive and negative in the contingencies. 'Foolish' action is often that which does not bother to read the conditions, or isn't subtle enough to pick up all of them and as a result can become clumsy and maladroit. This is spoken of as 'not reading the signs' and 'making matters worse'. Desire for sheer survival will ensure minimal interpretation of conditions in a situation but social and cultural realities will require a much deeper, richer, reading of conditions and contingencies to reflect an altogether more complex fabric.

To learn we must practise. But practising bad habits hinders us. There is a way to practise that opens us to learning, but this is not automatic. People may crow they have had 'years of experience and practice', yet they have learnt next to nothing. People can jettison top-down scientific models, even bottom-up 'working models', for the sake of learning from experience and practice, yet just get lost and go nowhere.

Reflection Point

JOURNEY

- *If you think of your life as a journey – what do you know now that you could not possibly have known at the beginning?*
- *What do you imagine you might know towards the end of your journey that you do not know now?*
- *List five things that have shifted within your personality since you were a child.*
- *Which parts of your journey have you needed to walk alone?*
- *What kind of people have you found make the best walking companions?*

What we need to practise, again and again, is how to get into what sports people and musicians call the zone. A few basic skills can perhaps be learned by mechanical rote but real expertise is more supple and hard to pin down. There is a set of attitudes, strategies, 'practices' that we can repeatedly try out that will put us in the zone where wisdom seeks wisdom, the zone where we can learn.

> ### The Streams in the Consulting Room
>
> **JOURNEY**
> In medium/long-term relational work the therapist must consciously hold the client through all stages of the journey and remain deeply aware of which stage the work is at and what might be coming next.
>
> Where are you currently in your journey as a therapist? What worries you about the next stage of the trip? What do you need to do to manage this next section successfully?
>
> A good way to conceptualise the therapy encounter is as a space of reflection, contemplation and knowing oneself during life's journey. The past and the future may be very present but the meeting between you and your client always happens in the here and now – the possibilities for change are always present too.

Unsupported, unguided beginners will try to make judgements using strict rules and features. With the cultivation of talent and a great deal of involved experience the beginner develops into an expert who sees intuitively what to do without applying rules and making judgements at all. Normally an expert does not unduly pause to reason or deliberate. She simply and spontaneously does what normally works and, quite naturally, it usually works again. We are all experts at many tasks and our everyday coping skills function smoothly and transparently so as to free us to be aware of other aspects of our lives where we are not so skilful.

> **Student Excerpt**
> One of my main discoveries across the course was my struggle to slow my judgement process down. The experiential exercises provided me with an opportunity to recognise my tendency towards interpreting a situation before even experiencing it on ground level. During the tree exercise I found myself trying to analyse why I had chosen to stand next to a particular tree even before taking time to really see it. It was in my nature to jump ahead to explanation mode.

So it is vital for someone wanting to move from the apprentice state to the state of expertise or mastery to accept that this journey takes a very long time – it cannot be rushed, there is no quick-and-easy fix. The young are often impatient in reacting to this truth. They are hungering for the destination when they have barely set out on the trip. This is entirely natural for them but those teaching and supporting must do everything they can to encourage them to appreciate why an understanding of the journey is at the heart of becoming a situated practitioner. In their journal keeping we ask students to record how they feel on their first day and later on the last day of their programme. In comparing the two they can see just how far they have come. There is no magic way to know how a journey will shape and change us when we set out and we must accept that with humility if we are to truly own the wisdom we will develop during the walk.

This is why the journey is one of the first streams: it is an attitude towards the trip that the student/apprentice must cultivate at the start – and not a bad one to hold on to for those of us further down the road – for in truth the journey never ends.

 The Key to the JOURNEY is accepting that the real joy comes from savouring the travelling rather than rushing towards the destination and from embracing the beauty of the divine paradox.

STREAM 4: ADVENTURE

Man cannot discover new oceans unless he has the courage to lose sight of the shore.

André Gide

The courage of which Gide speaks is a pre-requisite for the discovery of newness and is related to our sense of being on a journey in Stream 4: Adventure. When we talk of adventure in the situated context we could just as easily say 'letting go of anxiety'. In order to fully embrace a sense of adventure and discovery, to really inhabit the terrain, one must accept that anxiety will be a constant companion during the trip. If we do not realise this we may allow anxiety to make us turn back through fear and flee from the unknown. Why is it hard to be relational, and to negotiate, as a fundamental stance of being? Why is it often so hard to relinquish the illusion of control over things? Precisely because giving up this sense of control leaves us anxious as we venture into unfamiliar territory. And anxiety once it grabs hold of you can drag you along in its wake as though behind wild horses. Ask anyone in the grip of panic disorder, obsessive compulsive disorder or a crippling phobia how terrifying it is and how much it can control your life.

Even when it is not painted on such a large and dramatic canvas as this, anxiety can be devastating to our journey towards practising wisdom. It can be a like a rat, gnawing away, quietly in the dark, tearing to pieces any confidence you may build or any flash of inspiration that may come. If it stays in the unconscious realm it will often get the better of you. It has a thousand words of doom and destruction to lead you from the path through the forest, or to shelter under the first available rock to shield you from the harsh desert sun and stay there cowering, for fear of what might happen to you if you venture outside: 'It won't work', 'I'll get it wrong', 'This feels dangerous', 'What if I look foolish or incompetent or get out of my depth?', 'Maybe they will think less of me', 'It's too hard', 'It's too difficult', 'Easier to stay here with the devil you know'. Like a gloomy, frightened elf it will sit on your shoulder and nag at you to stay safe, convince you that you can't cope, that others won't like you, paint mental pictures in hideous detail about what will definitely go so awfully, terribly wrong. It can paralyse you and shrink your life if you let it.

For us there is only one way to manage your anxiety so that it does not run out of control like a cart down a hill. And that is to shine a torch in the elf's eyes, slap him about the head a little when he gets too hysterical and cultivate another voice which can help to calm, contain, support and encourage you when you are walking into the unknown. And we always are walking into the unknown in one way or another. To put it another way, we must face our fears head on, not run away screaming.

The Streams in the Consulting Room

ADVENTURE

Many clients come to therapy full of fear and nervousness – which is only natural. Our job is to act as a guide as they undertake this perilous adventure into the self and the psyche – the past and the future.

If we can encourage them to adopt an attitude of excited discovery rather than anxious apprehension right from the start it will help enormously – and naturally in order to model this way of being we have to feel it too.

Stay interested and curious as the journey begins with each new client – not closed in by our own self-doubt, apprehension or uncertainty.

The therapy process is like an adventure and as with every adventure there will be unexpected twists and turns. To hang on to a models-led approach seems like hanging on to a security blanket, as if this will keep everything neat and predictable. I know I felt that way at the beginning of my career as though following a models-led approach seemed less likely to let the client down (or to make me look foolish). With fool-proof frames that have been proved effective through years of research how one can go wrong as the therapist? I failed to see that forcing a specific model onto clients is not making the therapy safer and efficient; it simply neglects the fact that all clients have different needs.

When coming to therapy the client embarks on a journey, an adventure, travelling together with the therapist. And when going through that adventure together, the client needs a therapist that dares to think outside the box and tackle the unforeseen. Someone who has an open mind and is willing to try new approaches to meet the client's individual needs. It seems to me now that a good therapist is someone who can trust their well of knowledge instead of a 'fool-proof framework'. Even though situated action opens up the risk of not always getting everything 100 per cent right, I believe the Adventure stream makes an important point when claiming we must accept this fear of failure. The anxiety of letting yourself down, of letting the client down, will always be there. But if we accept that it is there, instead of hiding or running away from it, that is when we can truly attempt to help others face their own anxieties.

So why is this true of us? There are perhaps several answers to this, including the cultural bias of the West over centuries, and especially the tendency in higher education to value only the theoretical and ignore the existential. One answer our students come up with is that being models-led seems *safer and more powerful*; going into situations relatively naked seems exposed to far *greater uncertainty and jeopardy*. Expectation appears to guarantee a desired outcome, whereas situatedness guarantees nothing but puts everything at risk. Models promise absolute safety from uncertainty, from failure, from having to take personal responsibility for outcomes. This is why they are so seductive: stick with me, kid, follow the rules and you'll be OK, I'll look after you. Only a crazy person would choose to operate outside of the model, surely? In truth, in most spheres of human activity, people don't move outside of what models offer. They either choose the model consciously, are sometimes unaware that any other option exists as the model is all they know or, *in extremis*, have to accept the model under threat of force. In this sense models are bullies. They are also liars. They promise safety when what you really get is control and restriction.

Most of their enticements are illusory.

We are, when armed to the teeth with expectation, much more easily thrown by the unexpected and more frightened by that which cannot be anticipated. For the real world is full of surprises, and so are we, and so especially is the meeting of the two; it is actually a lot safer to be alert, ready, able to roll with the punches, when the unforeseen and unforeseeable turns up, as it always will. As Zen says, to be prepared for the emergent is to be better prepared, actually, than to be prepared only for the expected. So those of us who still hang on to the illusory safety of rigid model-led thinking must ask ourselves: why are we so afraid to let go and relinquish control? In trying to avoid the hurt, pain and mess of life do we also miss out on its richness, beauty, mystery and depth?

Reflection Point

ADVENTURE

- *Looking back, what have been the greatest adventures of your life so far?*
- *What mindset has served you best in fully encountering these experiences?*
- *Think of a time when you may have missed out on adventure through fear or worry about what others may think.*
- *What distinguishes the adventures missed from the ones taken?*

The reason we hang onto the lifebelts thrown to us by models when we first hit the freezing cold water is fear: fear of drowning, being overwhelmed, losing control and failing. It is existential angst showing up to challenge us in another guise. But as Emmy van Deurzen (1988, p.84) says, 'our goal should be to help clients face up to their anxiety rather than run away from it'. Life is anxiety provoking. This is true for us and for our clients. Any denial of that fact by us is to collude with our client's defence mechanisms. And if we are still trying to run, panic stricken, from that truth, how can we ever be of assistance to patients trying to look their own anxieties square in the face? The paralysing quality of powerful anxiety has been outlined in existential philosophy. Kierkegaard's (1945 [1843]) concept of Angst ('fear and trembling', 'the sickness unto death') is a mix of numinous apprehension and acute anguish, inescapable suffering suffused with fear (in Latin the term 'angine' means to be 'squeezed' or 'strangled'). Angst wakes us up to what death means for us personally, the precariousness of our situation in existence. From this, meaning-making becomes very personal – what matters to me – and it also becomes very existential: what proves itself as valid in the living of it, and especially what proves itself worthwhile in the face of death.

> To venture causes anxiety, but not to venture is to lose one's self… And to venture in the highest is precisely to be conscious of one's self.
>
> Søren Kierkegaard (1945)

Going into the wild is a risk. Working with risk, neither being cowardly nor arrogant toward it, is the mark of the adventurous person. A particular way of engaging risk is neither crippled by it, nor plays fast and loose with it, but finds a balance – there is the divine paradox again. The adventurous person has to decide how far to push it, when to hold back, when to go for broke. Taking risks would always be foolish unless we learn to read the terrain and learn from trying things out there.

 The Key to ADVENTURE is to embrace newness, feel the thrill of novelty and remember the excitement of childhood – don't allow fear to persuade you to sit down and not move forward.

CHAPTER 2
JUMPING IN

- Play and Exploration
- Inner Child
- Slowing Down
- Story and Metaphor
- Dialogue
- Space and Place

This set of streams consists of the core skills set that a competent therapeutic practitioner needs to build. In the Psychology and Counselling degree at the University of Roehampton (of which I am the Programme Convener) the first year introduces key theory, but focuses on building counselling skills through practice and self-exploration and reflecting on these core processes: before they happen, during and afterwards.

These streams need to be developed in the counsellor during training – so that they can bring a real awareness of them within themselves to their meetings with clients. More experienced practitioners will find they can continue deepening their appreciation of these streams throughout their career. Nervous beginners tend to move unconsciously towards the polar opposites – trying to be very serious and grown-up rather than playful and in touch with the inner child; rushing too fast instead of slowing down and really paying attention to phenomena. So it seems only right that in training and supervising them we must encourage the embrace of these streams to act as a counter-balance.

The 'Jumping In' streams also create much of the joy and spontaneity for those of us doing therapy – they keep us fresh, alive and on our toes; the best antidote to burn-out and slipping into repetitive models frameworks is to enjoy what we do – and the playful, exploratory mindset which is in no particular hurry is a great way to keep enjoyment alive.

This captures one particularly sweet paradox of situated action: in most models-led templates of the world, once you have mastered the rudiments you can forget them and move on to the more complicated (and interesting) stuff. In reality what happens is that the 'simple' stuff slips into our unconscious, implicit mind and happens without us needing to think about it. The cardiologist engaged in open heart surgery still has to breathe and digest their breakfast – luckily for the patient they don't need to consciously focus on this and lose concentration on the operation.

In psychotherapy (or any form of performance in an intersubjective field) this is only partly true. Certainly things become somewhat more automatic, our implicit mind and its tacit knowledge (what I call the well) supports us but we may still need to wrestle with the leap of faith before we walk through the door, remain highly aware of the journey with each new client, and strive to keep the sense of exploratory play alive with our five-hundredth client as with our fifth. In other words the streams do not diminish in importance as a resource as we become more experienced. We simply get more comfortable with them, they really get under our skin, settle deep into our practitioner bones and we can draw upon them more easily. Over time the tapestry gets richer, more detailed and more complex – combining play, empathy, improvisation and maturity, for example, might mean each stream bringing balance and subtlety to the others. From the outside it looks effortless – a beginner might look at us and feel they can never achieve this for themselves – they feel frozen by looking at the whole picture rather than staying with the experience of sewing each colourful thread.

If you are near the beginning, or teach those that are, or simply need reminding of this – these first steps are for you.

STREAM 5: PLAY AND EXPLORATION

> The major task of life is to remain actively creative, and that can only come from the ability to be in touch with the playful child deep in the personality…to hold onto the freshness of the child's encounter with the world.
>
> Heinz Kohut (1981)

Children delight in the mysterious, the unknown, the fresh and the new. Playing doesn't need to have a concrete goal or a certificate at the end of it. Indeed if it is too structured, rule-bound or controlled it loses its joyous and spontaneous nature. It is enjoyed and loved for its own sake. It is absorbing; you jump in and immerse yourself, forgetting what is going on around you. Do you remember as a child losing all track of time when you were playing and having Mum or Dad come to call you? Play is also incredibly creative and about as far away from the state of anxiety as it is possible to get. Humour is often built into the playing process. It must be fun. These are fantastic qualities for any therapist to model for their clients. If you've lost touch with it as you've grown up now is the time to start getting it back. Many of us do lose touch with our sense of playfulness as life progresses and pressures and responsibilities increase.

At times it can feel as though professional practice is designed to drain every drop of playfulness out of us – our training is long, hard, stressful and expensive; we have to prove our mastery of theory, technique and ourselves in therapy. We must abide by codes of ethics, professionally represent the Health Care Professions Council (British Psychological Society, United Kingdom Council of Psychotherapy, British Association of Counselling and Psychotherapy etc.), maintain liability insurance, undergo supervision, continuing professional development, perhaps move into teaching, research, practice supervision or management responsibilities. And that's before we throw in the other adult weights a modern, professional person must carry: mortgages, utility bills, perhaps childcare, rows with our partners, commuting and on and on…is it any wonder that the childlike state of simply playing frequently slips out of our grasp?

Despite the huge pressures which will continue to deplete us we must try our best to develop this stream within ourselves – in life generally but especially in therapy space. Remember discovery and exploration lie at the heart of situated practice – and playing is a super-rapid method of getting to that state. Play can produce a sense of 'hyper focus', or what Hungarian psychologist Mihaly Csikszentmihalyi (Csikszentmihalyi and Csikzentmihalyi 1988) calls absorption in 'Optimal Flow'.

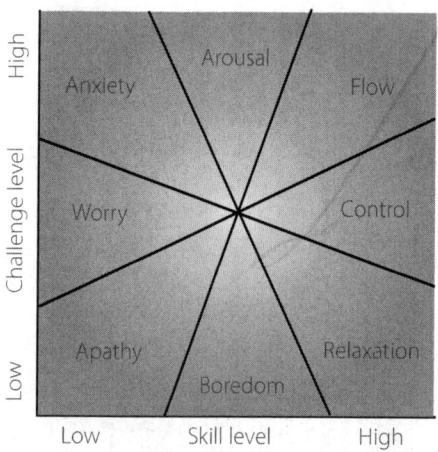

Csikszentmihalyi's flow model
Adapted from Csikszentmihalyi, M. and Csikszentmihalyi, I. (eds) (1988) Optimal Experience: Psychological Studies of Flow in Consciousness. *Cambridge: Cambridge University Press.*

He posits the idea that when both skill level and challenge level are at their highest we can enter 'optimal flow'. This is when we can seem expert to someone watching us undertake this activity; it is also, happily enough, when we enjoy ourselves the most. For beginners in any field it is only natural that, when we are possessed of a relatively low skill level if the level of challenge shoots up our anxiety level usually goes with it. We can marvel at the experienced practitioner smoothly inhabiting a state of optimal flow and feel terribly discouraged. Small children playing rarely feel such anxiety because they are not concerned with 'getting it right' but with enjoying the experience. Adults who try and make things too structured or rule-bound will suck all of the joy and interest out of a playful four-year-old. Instead the adults simply need to create a safe, permission-giving space in which the child's natural desire for exploration and imaginative play can unfold.

This absorption in ground-level activity means that the mind–body unity is gradually intensified to a near perfect, total, 'effortless' co-ordination. No pauses, no hesitancy, no need to stop and think or analyse and deliberate. Athletes call this 'getting into the zone'. An orchestra, playing their socks off, displays this beautifully. 'Everything comes together' and it all flows, seamlessly.

A football team where every member knows where others are in the space, and moves the ball magically to set up the scoring of goals, is also using this situated intelligence. So too is a good therapist, really in contact with the nuanced, subtle, hidden 'inner' movements of their client – as are humans any time they communicate with one another well. Creativity also taps this intelligence. It is neither the modern, atomistic 'intellect', nor even a more imaginative, speculative 'reason'. It scans the world both philosophically and realistically at once. It can only separate these later, in reflection after experience and action; but in experience and action, it encounters these two things as woven together in the way Heidegger described existential situatedness and embodiment in his landmark book, *Being and Time* (1962 [1927]).

So Discovery plays, gets absorbed in flow, and enters a trance-like focus. This too is required if we are to learn the way to be in a situation, in order to find the way through.

At times it will be hard to be in that play state. Sometimes the consequences of our next step in the terrain may feel too heavy. When we 'realise' what our experience is telling us – sometimes in a whisper, sometimes in a scream – we are shown an energy field where all the participants in it are mutually influencing each other, and are therefore inherently bound up with one another. I can look at you in order to experience nothing, and thus treat you as if you were nothing to do with me, and I will feel isolated. But as soon as I let myself experience you, it is a very different story. Who and what you are, your energy, goes into who and what I am, my energy, and just by being in the world you change my being in the world, because your presence is linked to my presence. It is thus neither objective, nor subjective. Rather, it is interpersonal, intersubjective (intersubjectivity is a stream we will explore more fully later in this book).

Reflection Point

PLAY

- The next time you are near a two-year-old just absorb how they encounter the world: fresh, excited, awestruck and emotional – curiosity knows no limits and the smallest things can be fascinating to them.
- Think about how you lost track of time when playing as a child – what did that state feel like?
- How often do you get to feel like that now?

So in therapy, as in life, the space between therapist and client becomes more productive, more healing when it retains an element of playfulness within it. Much of the content we deal with in our profession is heavy, pained and problematic. Our approach to the craft of therapy need not be: it can retain humour whilst honouring seriousness, it can play and explore rather than rushing ahead to an unsatisfactory, neat ending. Vitally it should create a place where the child within the client, both the parts that were wounded and the part that is magical, spontaneous and alive, feels able to emerge and bring back to life that sense of playful creativity which so many of us find slipping through our fingers like sand as the onerous duties and trials of adult life press forward.

The Streams in the Consulting Room

PLAY

If play is so vital why not have two-year-olds as psychotherapists?

Because another of the streams – balance – is vital here. The playful child in the therapist must be balanced with the containing adult.

For example, even after years of practice sometimes my absorption in the moment or my immersion in the world of this client means I lose track of time. Sticking to time boundaries is still challenging for me.

So the playful therapist contains a paradox – play must be present but cannot stay in charge; it must be contained.

Donald Winnicott, in his 1971 book, *Playing and Reality*, described the ideal therapy situation as one in which the therapist assists the client to re-enter a state of playfulness which could help them to transform painful aspects of the self into more creative and engaged ones. This process is deeply linked to the creativity stream which appears shortly. Marks-Tarlow (2012) outlines some of the key functions play performs for children including brain growth, self-regulation of both feelings and behaviour in social groups, building imaginative and symbolic representation capabilities, practising meaning-making and enhancing language and narrative skills (p.88). Primarily children play because it is great fun and yet all these vital skills are being promoted under the radar whilst they are enjoying themselves. Adults who believe that play is wasted time and that the only proper learning takes place in schoolrooms or by doing homework are horribly mistaken. Knowing, as we do, that the refiguring of some of the neural networks in the client's right brain can occur in longer-term relational psychotherapy (see Badenoch 2008 and Montgomery 2013) there are wholly valid 'scientific' reasons why counselling space can embrace playfulness.

To play is to explore, to try out, to become absorbed and to enter a sense of timeless flow – the situated practitioner needs all these to flourish. To really engage in play and to assist the client to do so we need to embrace the inner child – and that is the next stream.

The Key to PLAY is letting go of expectation and allowing oneself to be absorbed in the here-and-now (just keep one eye on the clock!)

STREAM 6: INNER CHILD

Classical psychoanalysis calls them defence mechanisms: denial, displacement, intellectualisation, humour, repression and so on. Over the years I have come to call these defence mechanisms survival strategies. When we arrive into our families as babies, toddlers and small children we are wholly dependent on the adults around us to feed and clothe us, to keep us warm and not hurt us physically nor, it is hoped, hurt us too much emotionally. It takes a good while for us to develop even small competencies in self-regulation, walking, talking and acting independently. The human child is fairly helpless for a remarkably long time when compared to most other animals.

I often joke with my students that a child born into a difficult family cannot simply announce that they can no longer bear it, they are moving down the street, please forward my pocket money via my solicitors. This usually gets a laugh – but in reality it isn't funny. The family – or the individual – we get, we are largely stuck with until we are grown up – and even then we may carry them internally for the rest of our life. Unless they seriously abuse us nobody else will intervene (and sadly not even then in many cases). The growing child has to learn to make do with what they have, to work with the material to hand. In other words, the child has to largely adapt to what is expected of them. Parents make it clear in thousands of very subtle (and sometimes less subtle) ways what they want the child to be, how much they can cope with, whether they feel over or under-stimulated by this child. Is this child truly loved, accepted as who they are, are they made to feel welcome in this world? In object relations theory when the answers to those questions are largely yes, the child is said to be receiving 'good mirroring'. In person-centred theory we talk about 'conditions of worth'. When the child looks into the face of their primary caregiver (in most instances, mother) do they really see what Donald Winnicott called 'the gleam in the mother's eye'? This gleam cannot be faked. Are they pleased to see us, do we sense affection, joy and pleasure from them at our very presence? As in any other relationship do we feel wanted, accepted, valued and welcomed? Am I a worthwhile person, am I loved? And since this is our very first experience of a growing relationship the responses we get from our first 'other' matter enormously in shaping how we see ourselves and whether we experience the world as a largely hostile, cold and attacking place or one that is broadly warm, safe and accepting of who we are. My sense of me is largely taken in from how I am seen by my first 'others'.

Parts of us may seem to arouse envy, hostility, distance or coldness in this other person, particularly when we start to really become aware of ourselves as a separate individual. We may realise that these parts seem to provoke negative feelings in others, whilst different aspects of us bring about positive responses. It's only natural that most children tend to play up the parts evoking positive responses whilst trying to hide parts that elicit mostly negative responses. I sometimes say to clients that we shove the bits of the self that the world seems to like out to the front of the stage to keep the audience clapping. Meanwhile the parts that we are scared of, ashamed of or feel uncomfortable with lurk behind the curtains, only emerging when we are angry, stressed or alone — usually making us love them even less. Nobody who is psychologically well enjoys having the crowd jeer and boo at their performance. And we all perform the self to the world audience every day.

What the child imagines may be something intrinsically broken in them, may be driven by the angry negative emotions of the parents. In the child's mind they may feel responsible for a mummy that seems to be frequently unhappy or a daddy that goes away all the time. A small child will try to work out: what is it I'm doing that causes unhappy mummy or abandoning daddy to show up in my world? Experiencing an unhappy or angry or distant or chaotic mum, or a depressed or violent or critical, preoccupied dad is far less preferable than the mother or father who may be more kind, tolerant, loving and present. The child tries to maximise the good parental presence and minimise the bad.

Some of us had a broadly good childhood and the ways in which we were shaped, wounded, damaged or pressurised by those around us may have been relatively subtle. This doesn't mean they don't have very profound effects on our personality even if to the rest of the world it may have seemed things were broadly all right. Many of these clients, when they first come into psychotherapy, will report enthusiastically that they had a positive, happy, good childhood and cannot understand why they now react in certain ways as adults when they had nothing but joy and pleasure and happiness when they were little.

The other group of children experienced wounding in childhood that is all too obvious. Parents may have been hostile, cruel, abandoning – they may have died or the family may have broken up. The child may have been physically, emotionally and sexually abused or constantly neglected. The parents may have been addicted or drunk. They may have been working out the dark wounding of their own childhoods on this vulnerable baby. Here the survival strategies the child had to adopt may have been more severe and taken place much earlier. In films of mother–child attachment behaviour in the early months of the baby's life we can see such gross defensive responses to over-intrusive or highly anxious mothers. The baby will turn their head away and remove all eye contact. If the mother's attunement to the baby's behavioural cues is especially poor the infant may do this much of the time. They cannot fight (or flight), so they freeze, they disassociate from this unpleasant stimulus. If the young girl has to learn to fight, or to be angry and hostile in order to survive, that's what she will do. If the young boy has to learn to be quiet and compliant and give the parent what they want in order to survive that's what he will do too. Children who could never predict when Mum or Dad might be cruel, violent or distant towards them have a particularly tough time.

I keep a very close watch for the survival strategies carried from childhood. Not all of these will be maladaptive – some ways of self-soothing or of coping under emotional pressure can be quite functional (learning to walk away from conflict, learning to calm ourselves down and take time-out or asking for what we need from others). These adaptive survival strategies usually lead to things improving or being less painful than they were before. They certainly don't damage things further or increase the level of conflict with other people, leaving us feeling worse off than when we started.

However, it is the negative, maladaptive survival strategies that usually bring the person into therapy in the first place. What may have been appropriate for a rather naive and limited child to adopt as survival strategies may not work so well for an adult. Because these strategies have been in place for a while, they are often embedded and largely unconscious and they tend to be quite sticky and difficult to shift. I often liken it to helping a soldier realise that they are no longer fighting on the battlefield and that the war is over. The simplistic weapons that were needed to survive childhood must be put down.

Initially many clients are sceptical of the whole idea of the inner child. During our very busy adult lives we strive to be grown-up, juggling heavy responsibilities around work, relationships, finances and often children. Usually by the time they come to psychotherapy something in this ongoing stressful plate spinning is breaking down: anxiety, depression, relationship problems, feeling empty, loneliness or a loss of meaning in life, may have started to overwhelm the person and make them feel sad, lost, frightened or angry.

So when I first mention the inner child some see it as a Californian new-age sort of idea, particularly men. Indeed I was dubious myself when I first came across this notion 20 years ago. Over this time I have become deeply convinced that the living presence of the inner child inside the adult really shapes much of our emotional health, well-being and happiness in life (or lack thereof). The inner child represents a storehouse of memories, feelings, beliefs, unprocessed trauma and survival strategies that were shaped and adapted during very early childhood and then nuanced, rehearsed and embedded during adolescence and early adulthood.

> ### Reflection Point
>
> **INNER CHILD**
>
> - Take a moment to recall what your life was like when you were five years old.
> - Where did you live? Whom did you love? Who really loved you? Which parts of life were working? What may have caused your little one sadness, exclusion, fear or pain?
> - What aspects of that small child still live on inside you?
> - Your inner child is more likely to show up when you are disregulated: lonely, angry, scared, tired or ecstatic, excited or falling in love.
> - What does it feel like when they do?

We know within ourselves when the inner child is present. There are two main forms – firstly, *the wounded child*, who carries the difficult and painful feelings, memories and beliefs of specific parts of the self that have become arrested. When the child was unable to cope psychologically with what was going on around them they may have dissociated from, repressed or tried to escape from the emotional pain. Powerful experiences of feeling rejected, angry, mocked, unlovable or physically unsafe may have overwhelmed the child's nervous system and brain functioning, and defence mechanisms (survival strategies), ways of adapting to this difficult environment, started to emerge. There is now a huge amount of work on the long-term effects on the child of being exposed to complex trauma with which every practitioner needs to familiarise themselves (Badenoch 2008; Cozolino 2010; de Zulueta 2006; Montgomery 2013; Sanderson 2013).

The second part of the inner child is extraordinarily important: *the wonder child* or *the magical child*. This inner child expresses joy, happiness, creativity, play and love. They love to explore, to get silly, to be playful, get creativity flowing and to be the receiver of lots of warm admiration, love and support. For those of us carrying deep wounding, the wonder child may have been repressed by adults, or learned to suppress itself in response to what they believed the adults around them wanted. Many clients that come to my consulting room have really lost touch with the wonder child within them. Real feelings of spontaneity, joy, playfulness and wonder are often very flat and sometimes non-existent. If we think of the child inside them as being the one driving the car of their life, more often than not it's the wounded child at the wheel of the car rather than the wonder child. No wonder they are stuck in negative thinking, beliefs and responses – which can lead to them becoming ill, unhappy and despondent and losing hope.

My job as a psychotherapist, in a nutshell, is to lead this person through a corrective relational experience whereby the wounded inner child can heal and the wonder child can be released and start to take more positive control of their life. The children that emerge into the consulting room vary enormously: some say nothing and try to hide. Others cling to the adult/parental part of the client's psyche, don't want to let them go and can barely stop talking because they have so much to say after so many years of being silenced. During guided imagery work one woman who was an alcoholic and had an alcoholic mother found her six-year-old girl sitting in a cellar, completely bare of furnishings and toys, yet filled with empty wine bottles.

Another client had arrived in therapy with deep obsessive-compulsive issues and severe worries about her expression of sexuality, and found her child at the age of four sitting very consciously with her legs drawn together, because her extremely religious mother had told her that what was between her legs was disgusting and never to be shown to the world. This particular lady was extraordinarily shocked and surprised to find that her inner child was expressing this fear which had been very secret.

Some clients feel loving protectiveness towards their internal children straightaway. Others struggle to feel any connection to, or compassion for, that small child. The first inner child we meet is usually between two and eight. I hear clients aiming vicious negative self-talk towards themselves and their inner child. Most do this unconsciously and when it's pointed out to them many are horrified. One man who was having issues with his partner, and failing to perform sexually in the way that he wanted, was totally condemning of himself as a man and often described himself as pathetic, useless and awful.

I sometimes ask the client to imagine that three or four-year-old self sitting in a small chair next to my therapist chair. I ask them to repeat the same harsh negative self-talk at the child. In most cases they struggle to do this and cannot even imagine repeating such things to any child, let alone their own. They find it hard to imagine they are capable of doing this. And yet in many cases for 20, 30, 40 years or more there has been a daily diet of this bile directed towards the child part of the self. Many of these bad messages will have originated outside the child, but have been internalised so successfully and rehearsed so often down the years they have come to feel like the secret truth about the self. It makes living inside their skin and their mind a tough place to be.

Now these exercises are not intended to make the client feel guilty or bad about what they've been doing – there is more than enough of that washing around already. However, it's important that they come to realise what psychological, emotional and physical impacts they are having on themselves by continuing to engage in this constant negative self-talk abuse and self-degradation. An effective way to manage this is to invite the client, if they can, to get hold of a photograph (or photographs) depicting themselves at that inner child age and bring it to therapy. We look at it together and see how they respond to that child. Frequently we find that powerful memories emerge during such exercises.

I usually encourage them to keep this photograph visible in their home for a while. When they catch themselves engaging in this negative talk I suggest that they look at the innocence and beauty of that child's face, and remind themselves that negative self-talk can only be damaging. Many clients report that it reminds them how vulnerable they are and how much they need compassion from themselves rather than constant hostility – much Buddhist and Mindfulness practice focuses on such loving-kindness meditations towards self and others. We can gradually learn to treat ourselves more gently and compassionately if we practise holding the inner child in our conscious awareness. If I find myself being very harsh, or driving myself too hard, feeling too guilty or blaming myself too much – I take time to remind myself that this little fellow is still alive inside of me. And it's my responsibility to take care of him in the best way I can. This is where the notion of reparenting the self comes from; it may originate in the reparative aspects of the therapeutic relationship but once internalised the client can function as a much better parent to themselves.

Some clients, like Laura, initially find it very difficult to feel anything like compassion towards the inner child. Laura had come from a very damaged and chaotic family where her mother told Laura that she was a useless burden, unlovable, whom no one would ever really want. As a result, the adult Laura's reaction to her inner child in our psychotherapy sessions was fearful and hostile. She angrily told me that she'd spent 35 years trying to get away from this little bitch and that she didn't want her anywhere near her. Many of her survival strategies and habitual behaviours were concerned with escaping this powerless child who felt that she was worth nothing. Laura was genuinely torn: realising that this inner child could never be fully gotten rid of, and yet feeling absolute terror at the idea of embracing this child back into her life. The re-experiencing of the shame and humiliation of that small girl in the here and now felt unbearable.

However, after nearly two years of working with this woman things were completely transformed from a point where this girl was somebody she wanted at arm's length, and even entertained fantasies of trying to kill, to the inner child taking centre stage in her life. She learned how to take care of herself at a far more effective and profound level. One way we did this was to imagine each night tucking this small child into bed alongside her and whispering good night, wishing her sweet dreams and saying that she would be happy to see her in the morning. This rarely happened in actual childhood; her parents were often drinking, angry and chaotic. Bedtime stories, cuddles and a gentle calming presence were things she learned to do without as a little girl. Gradually, over many months, she learned how to begin bringing a soothing, calming and containing energy to herself as an adult. It was a slow process, as all repairing of the seriously wounded inner child is slow, but it was valuable, effective and profound nevertheless.

In my experience, the dominant sub-personalities tend to represent polarities of the personality. For example, when working with Rita, a rather straight-laced barrister in her late thirties, it became clear that two strong sides of this woman's personality existed. One was Little Miss Rules. This character was obsessive, somewhat compulsive, very duty-bound and guilt-prone, highly anxious over not working hard enough or letting other people down. She carried massive guilt over an ex-boyfriend's suicide.

The other sub-personality was Miss Fuck You. She emerged occasionally when Rita was under a lot of pressure; she was sick of taking care of other people's needs and worrying about them. Miss Fuck You liked to drink, take drugs, have lots of casual sex and didn't want to think about consequences or how her behaviour impacted others. To use psychological jargon, we could say that Little Miss Rules had an excessively external locus of evaluation. Miss Fuck You, on the other hand, had an extremely internal locus of evaluation. The first personality is overly concerned with the rules of other people, whereas the second personality fantasises about taking no notice whatsoever of others. Rita had spent 20 years swinging backwards and forwards between these two extremes. Neither served her well, but she found it extremely difficult to move towards a healthier middle ground. A quick word of caution: this type of 'parts' work (inner child or sub-personality exercises) is not suitable for anyone currently experiencing psychotic episodes or with a background of dissociative identity disorder (DID) or schizophrenia.

The Streams in the Consulting Room

INNER CHILD

There is no point doing inner child work with clients until they are relaxed, present, feeling safe with you and open to such internal exploration.

The wounded parts of the child that show up in adult defences, neurotic symptomology and relationship conflicts have been in place a long time – usually very well defended and convinced that their view of the world is the right one.

To support this part to come into the room and move towards healing takes sensitivity, patience and loving compassion from the therapist. The deepest and most permanent change in the personality structure is possible once they do.

Now this may seem fairly obvious, but the usual next stage is to get these different parts of the self to talk to one another. To do this, I normally employ a variety of techniques from Gestalt therapy. The client sits in one chair and tries to embody one particular sub-personality – for most it is surprisingly easy. If that part of self came to represent unexpressed anger, abandonment, lust or disagreement they get into the energy associated with it and give it some expression. Often the opposing part of self tries to keep these difficult feelings under control. We could say that these represent aspects of the real self and of the false self – one represents the mask of acceptability that we try to present within society, while the other represents the boiling unconscious emotions which we are frequently taught to hide. For some of us as children it was simply not safe to reveal these underlying emotions. Part of the successful learning we did growing up was to keep these difficult feelings hidden from view. In many ways, we learn this split from our parents. Mothers and fathers often strive to keep their real feelings hidden from their children because they believe that this will protect them. At times, they tell their children that they are not upset or angry or afraid in order to try and reassure. However, particularly for younger children, this may be confusing and gives the message that some feelings are not talked about or acknowledged. Thankfully fewer families stick to these rules today but in the recent past this model was all too common.

For Rita she was eventually able to feel what she had only been able to intellectualise previously: that neither of these extreme sub-personalities was helping provide a stable, happy life. The middle ground for her was practising being more assertive and ensuring her child was listened to when she felt overburdened with responsibility. She found that by building more regular valves for letting off steam and remembering to play and take care of her needs, the periodic reckless explosions of Miss Fuck You began to calm down.

 The first Key to the INNER CHILD in therapy is trust – knowing that this new adult will not merely reproduce the childhood conditions which first shamed, angered, excluded or hurt them – but offer something different that can be safely internalised. The second Key is time – this process cannot be rushed, although it doesn't need to take years either.

STREAM 7: SLOWING DOWN

The best work in psychoanalysis comes when you are fairly old. Physicists do their best work at 20, Mathematicians at 19. But in depth psychology you have to live long enough to get close to the experience and yet stay detached from it. There are two psychologies… one is immersed in experience – mysticism and excitement and cure through love…and then the totally detached ones. Neither is absolutely right. You have to do both at the same time.

Heinz Kohut (1977)

To make sense of the lay of the land we usually need to experience and do things repeatedly – as Aristotle said, phronesis is the 'fruit of years' (1953, p.124). To those who privilege models-led ways of working this may suggest blind, rote-like ways of learning sets of rules and conditions that we must apply. Where rigid theory becomes 100-page rulebooks we can see someone trying to remove the trying out, making mistakes and learning from the ground elements of developing expertise. The rulebook says we must learn from someone else's conclusions about operating well in the territory – never from our own. The longer ago the rulebook was codified the more problematic this becomes.

Models tend to make the promise that they can be a shortcut on this journey – a quick fix, sparing you from some of the long grind through the territory. As humanity has recognised for thousands of years through the use of the master/apprentice relationship you need to give yourself the gift of time to fully inhabit a new role. Being an apprentice is a noble thing! People today are often non-humble and impatient; they want to leap straight to the expert stage. A good wine must ferment and ripen. We move through the territory initially guided strongly by others but needing them less and less as we attain mastery. This is true for children and their parents, therapists and their mentors and – of course – for clients and their therapists.

Thus, through much practising, we learn what it is to divest ourselves of *a priori* ideas and emotions, to think on our feet, to juggle several things at once, to be spontaneous, and to improvise. We get used to the wave in its very freshness and surprise, so we get very much more adept at doing things with its help. But even the expert surfer can fall off the board by losing some of their built-up rapport with the wave.

The Streams in the Consulting Room

SLOWING DOWN

Much publicly funded therapy is moving towards ever shorter contracts. The pressure to cure fast comes from both the client and from providers.

This stream says that if we do not slow down, we will miss too much of the client's complex and unique story – and healing is in danger of becoming impersonal and superficial.

Slowing down helps both parties to uncover layers of meaning, recover gradually and to pay attention to detail.

It would be naive to pretend the forces of speed are not crowding in all around us – but try and hold them back for a short while whenever you can.

It must also be noted that sometimes novices do extraordinary things because, with so little knowledge, they sometimes tap directly into the wave, trusting and co-operating with it because they have no other option. Experts sometimes, because of having so much knowledge, limit what the wave might do. One of our students, a football coach, explored this idea:

Student Excerpt

The conscious understanding of what you can do, can inhibit performance. Footballers that are instinctive by nature probably cannot describe what they are meant to do; they just have the ability to do it. This supports the theory of learning through experience. Players that are programmed to react in a certain way in specific situations will probably lose their instinctive nature. In general the most successful, creative and instinctive footballers in the world come from Brazil. Brazil has high levels of deprivation and an unstructured football environment. Youngsters learn their trade on the streets and the beaches largely without the influence of adults and coaches. These young players are learning in the situated mode. This has produced some of the world's finest footballers.

This is why, when out of the situation, we think we know nothing. We cannot hold it in our conscious head, cannot remember it all consciously. Put us back in the situation and suddenly it is there again. We know it below the neck, in the body. Experts are strong both in the familiar, and in the unfamiliar. Rafael Nadal does not hit his impossible shots just by picking up a tennis racquet and waiting for inspiration to lift him. Some amateurs under-estimate 'what it takes' to get used to dealing with the unfamiliar in specific terrain.

An example: a party of young people in the summer of 2007 ventured into the French Alps on a pleasant day, but found themselves out of their depth higher up. All of them died. It transpired that no one in the party had ever done any serious mountain climbing. No one had appropriate clothing and boots, food or water, or tools such as rope, hammers or crampons. This sad event is a warning to respect the terrain we are going into; although beginners can have breakthroughs and experts can lose their 'touch', it remains true that much time must be spent, and much effort expended, in learning what to do in the terrain. It is no good trying to walk before crawling, or trying to run before walking, or trying to fly without running. Situated functioning improves by degrees, as we practise it. In part, this is because we consciously relate to the situated process better, but it is also down to the situated process unconsciously connecting more fully to the terrain. We must do our homework. Not studying a book gives no permission not to study the terrain. The seeming effortlessness of situated functioning at its peak requires much sweat, a few tears, and even a splash of blood, to get there.

> ### Reflection Point
>
> **SLOWING DOWN**
> *The modern world privileges speed, novelty and disposability. For perfectly understandable reasons many of us get caught up in this exhausting rush.*
>
> *Meditation and mindfulness help us to slow down, be present in the here-and-now moment and clear our mind so that we can be better aware of ourselves and the intricate beauty of the world around us and within us.*
>
> *Taking time to be with your internal world and switch off from the external maelstrom of techno stimuli and human demands is vital in sustaining our well-being.*

Therefore the situated practitioner requires extraordinary patience – not just in terms of their own journey towards hopeful mastery, but in working at being truly patient every time we undertake a new journey with a client. For the more experienced it can be rather tempting to diagnose the person very early on, as you recognise certain patterns having seen them many times before. Indeed you may have a solid idea of the nature of this person's psychological troubles, something of what caused them and some strong notions of the work required for these to change. And yet these thoughts – whilst broadly relevant – can never be person-specific. The levels of intricacy, complexity and uniqueness relating to this one human being only deepen as time goes on and eventually they become like no other client you ever had. We can only regard others as a homogenous mass from a distance; the closer we get to each person the more extraordinary they are, the more they become completely themselves, an individual unlike any one of the other seven billion people on the planet. To complete this journey from the generic to the specific takes time and that can only happen when we are patient and slow down. In many ways this is the antithesis of the modern world, where everything is ever more rapid, instant and disposable. Good therapy – like a good relationship – must not be like this and as ethical practitioners we must resist, as best we can, the onward rushing tide of speed.

In learning to slow down and take time we notice things we may have missed before, we open ourselves up to myriad possibilities that rapid diagnosis and decision making may deny us. In a world that moves at an ever faster pace this stream requires us to be courageous to stick to this slower pace of discovery and learning – spending months or years in a new land offers much deeper possibility for true understanding than the three-days highlights tour. To slow down we must resist the pressure to rush and to trust that we will get there in the end, even as we feel that we have to get there right now.

 The Key to SLOWING DOWN is resistance – resisting the internal voice which says you must figure everything out right now if you are a halfway decent therapist; the external pressures (money, politics and organisational requirements) which want solutions and cures faster and cheaper than ever before and the fear of the suffering client, who perhaps feels unable to undergo the longish haul that leads to real change, but wants you to provide the quick fix immediately.

STREAM 8: STORY AND METAPHOR

> The human story does not always unfold like a mathematical calculation on the principle that two and two make four. Sometimes in life they make five or minus three; and sometimes the blackboard topples down in the middle of the sum and leaves the class in disorder and the pedagogue with a black eye.
>
> Winston Churchill (cited in Czarnomski 1956, p.59)

As Churchill knew, the narrative structure of a human life is never simple or predictable, each one of us has a deep and intricate story inside us that separates us from each of the other seven billion people currently alive on this planet. And yet there is much that binds us together as we have already seen. Our personal story separates us from everyone else yet the sharing of stories draws us closer together. An understanding of this paradox is inherent in recognising the centrality of story and narrative in the shaping of human experience, history and society. The use of metaphor, story and narrative is an invaluable source of enlightenment in working with clients.

Only the narrative form with its array of drama, recurrent figures, adventures, clashes and reversals of fortune conveys with any veracity all that human beings experience on the ground. Stories have limits within which even heroes must operate, plots, symbols and images, and crucially the change that comes to protagonists and what they learn. We tell each other stories all the time to try to communicate our human experience in both its difference and commonality. Such stories, whether ordinary or extraordinary, are not mere photographic representations of the experiential domain, nor are they arbitrary constructions of it. They are conversations between us and existence in which each side 'gets their say', and something genuine is arrived at through the pressure exerted by both. Good stories always carry some universal truth about human existence.

Our Self-Story

The first-person narrative through which we define our identity is based on memories, perceptions of our history, our present life, our roles in various social and personal settings and our relationships. These stories are often told to others and more frequently to ourselves with recurring themes and dominant concepts. We often project this narrative into an assumed future – making up a story and then acting as though it is true. People are driven by this process for much of their life – usually unconsciously, and people who have become trapped by their life story are frequent visitors to the consulting room.

Ryan is a 23-year-old man, the second child in a chaotic family, where his father was frequently absent and his mother was often nervous, possessive and jealous. His father eventually left and his mother was finally sectioned. When Ryan was conceived the marriage was on the point of breaking up. His mother confessed to him when he was aged five that she had become pregnant to try and hold his father within the relationship. Ryan's story had been prepared for him before he even arrived in this world. His job was to soothe and mend things, to make it all right for everybody else. We came to label this as his 'impossible task', calming the chaos of his fractured family. Ryan tried desperately as a small boy to fulfil his role, often attempting to physically separate his warring parents and then providing a shoulder to cry on for his distraught mother. Not surprisingly he came to see himself as a failure for not preventing all this pain and gradually grew very out of touch with his own feelings, needs and choices, so busy was he in trying to interpret what was happening inside everyone else.

As he grew up the internalisation of this emotional chaos left him riddled with neurotic anxiety which eventually manifested as an obsessive thought disorder which plagued him for over ten years. During therapy Ryan was helped to see that this story of his function in life was given to him by someone else: it was the defining truth of who he was. Gradually he learned to claim back some space for his own life and needs, to separate and be himself by creating a new story.

Reflection Point

STORY

- *If your life was a story what do you feel would be the central themes?*
- *Do you feel like the author of your story?*
- *Who authored your story when you were a child? What themes did they add of their own?*
- *If the next five years were the next chapter in the story of your life what would you want it to be about?*

Human beings are interpreting beings – we are active in the interpretation of our experiences as we live our lives. The meanings derived in this process are not neutral in their effect on our lives, but really effect the steps we take. Our story or self-narrative determines which aspects of our lived experience gets expressed. Our stories actually shape our lives and embrace our lives. (White 1995, p.22)

Story, metaphor and narrative help us to make better sense of our multiple journeys through the territory. Each time we return, the story familiarises us with what has gone before. Our sense of needing to find out what happens next keeps us going at times when momentum stalls. It is vital for situated therapists to be clear on the importance of story, both in shaping the clients' original psychopathology and in the repair of the self.

The Streams in the Consulting Room

STORY

We have to stay intrigued when a client walks through the door – like turning to the first page of a long and complex book – there is pleasure in allowing the stories to unfold and the intricacies appear.

Yet we are not a passive reader – we engage and pay attention, particularly to metaphors which appear early in the work. These often evolve into a shared currency that allows the client to feel heard, understood and as though they matter to you.

They also offer a mental and emotional anchor for the client between sessions and when therapy finishes.

There is something endlessly fascinating – at times beautiful, at times horrifying – about the human condition and the therapist needs to remain open and alive to the story in all its myriad forms.

Therapy works when people are able to move beyond merely seeing themselves as the product of a set of narratives written in childhood by others about who they are and how they must act in the world. Often people come to therapy feeling stuck in one storied version of reality, as its victim, doomed to continually act out the same patterns and scripts. John Bowlby (1997) talks of an internalised working model of relationships. What this usually means is that people reach adulthood with a strong set of beliefs, defences and survival strategies around how they expect the world to treat them and how they believe they must be in order to be accepted, loved and respected. The flip side of this is that certain sides of self are then denied, shut off or feared – part of the real self goes underground because we come to think that it is too unpleasant, dislikeable, unlovable or overwhelming for other people.

The therapy journey often involves bringing this shadow side of self back into the light and learning to love it again. In doing this clients are able to transcend the earlier limiting story they carry about life and themselves, to see it for what it is: only one version of a life story predominantly fashioned by others to fit around their neurosis and limitations. The truly liberating period comes when they start to feel that they can be the main writers of the next chapters of their story. As Jung (1955, p.54) argues 'nothing has a stronger influence psychologically on their environment and especially on their children than the unlived life of the parent'. If mother and father were the authors of the early chapters of life, we aim for them to take over as the active creators of the rest of their book.

We use the streams of situatedness as tools to get us deeply immersed within the terrain, to fully experience its uniqueness and meaning. However we need to be wary of saying *the* terrain. There is, of course, not just one territory. Each new client is new terrain. And each session is a further visit to that terrain. Both you and the client will be getting to know the land more thoroughly each time. The client has lived in the territory for a lifetime. However, they have blind spots, perhaps areas which originally scared or overwhelmed them, which they choose to ignore. And, sometimes, parts of their own terrain they have forgotten about altogether. Clients are experts in some parts of the self and yet total novices in others.

It is tempting to think of the journey into the territory of a new client as a linear journey, some kind of quest for the holy grail of the person's psyche. In my experience, however, it is rarely so clear-cut. The journey is normally more of a circular return, often over and over again, to the same territory of the client's early developmental and relational experience and how that plays out in their current life and here in the room with you.

This is where the use of imagery, metaphor and narrative becomes extraordinarily powerful. Sometimes a single image can become a visual metaphor for a complex set of memories, feelings and beliefs. Once established between you it can be returned to repeatedly. In the terrain it becomes a marker, a signpost, and over time it can serve as a central reference point which starts to connect up with other metaphorical imagery. Eventually this can begin the co-construction of the person's central life story or narrative. It often amazes me how powerful and tenacious these metaphors can be – a client recently returned to work with me following a divorce. It has been six years since we last met. In his first session upon returning he brought up a metaphor related to parts of the self – connected to a mouse and a rat – he had used to chart his progress in the long gap since our last meeting. I was astonished to learn that something that formed part of our work together many years before still had a living presence within him.

Fiona was a woman in her mid-thirties who grew up with an alcoholic mother and a father who left the family when she was three years old. As an adult she displayed a typical symbiotic relational style. Part of her longed for closeness and merger yet many of her deepest memories of relationship were about being pulled into the dark, chaotic orbit of another and being unable to escape. At times it felt easier to be alone and independent, if lonely, rather than experiencing that terror of engulfment. Throughout most of her adult life she had contracted against her need for closeness and convinced herself she didn't want it whilst simultaneously feeling crushed by the loneliness of her existence. As her new relationship with Peter developed this terror would often return and she would think of breaking up each time a difficulty occurred. This was deeply frustrating to her and she worried she would always be alone.

One day in session, trying to attune to how this felt, I offered the image of sitting in a plane with your hand hovering just above the ejector seat button, waiting to hit it at the first sign of danger. This resonated closely with Fiona's experience. We returned to this idea frequently and she recognised it herself in interactions with Peter. Eventually she uncovered a belief that she would be unable to leave the relationship once it got past a certain point – just as she had been trapped in childhood with her mother's chaos and neglect. We developed the imagery so that she still had the ejector button and could use it at any time but now it was behind glass with a key to unlock it. This began to reinforce the idea that she was no longer a defenceless child unable to leave when things were unbearable but a resourceful adult who could recognise when she had had enough. This enabled Fiona to relax enough so that the relationship could develop more easily. Two months after our work together ended I had an email from Fiona: now living with Peter, planning their marriage and thinking of having children. She had amazed herself that by uncovering and releasing these old beliefs her experience of being with others had transformed itself.

 The Key to STORY is having a sense of the big picture – how the here and now fits in with the back then and the time still to come. It is a balancing stream to IMMERSION and a companion one to the JOURNEY.

STREAM 9: DIALOGUE

In the experience of dialogue, there is constituted between the other person and myself a common ground; my thought and his are interwoven into a single fabric, my words and those of my interlocutor are called forth by the stage of the discussion, and they are inserted into a shared operation of which neither of us is the creator. We have here a dual being, where the other is for me no longer a mere bit of behaviour in my transcendental field, nor I in his; we are collaborators for each other in consummate reciprocity.

M. Merleau-Ponty (2013, p.354)

Intersubjectivity: everything is dialogue, all is relationship
Based on the work of his mentor, Edmund Husserl, Jose Ortega y Gasset, in his important work, *Man and People* (1957), points out

> the radical solitude of human life, the being of man, does not then consist in there really being nothing except himself. Quite the contrary – there is nothing less than the universe, with all it contains. There is, then, an infinity of things but – there it is! – amid them Man

in his radical reality is alone – alone with them. And since among these things there are other human beings, he is *alone with* them too.

Klugman (2001) helps us to locate this idea within object relational therapeutic practice. He suggests that therapists should bring into focus at all times '*both* the individual's world of inner experience *and* its embeddedness with other such worlds' (Stolorow and Atwood 1992). Intersubjectivity theory introduces the concept of an *intersubjective field* in which both parties contribute and which both help to co-create. I have mentioned this concept already but it is so central to situated practice that I need to expand upon it.

No two intersubjective fields will be the same and indeed, one can argue that a new intersubjective space is created each time two people interact. Stephen Mitchell (2000) describes the increasing analytic acceptance of this idea as the 'relational turn' (p.57). This acknowledges that 'subjectivity always develops in the context of intersubjectivity' (Mitchell 2000, p.57). Take gender identity as an example. With regard to a boy's developing sense of maleness we can say that this does not develop merely inside of himself but in relation with and in reaction to the ways of being male he sees around him and, importantly, in reaction to the commentary and judgement placed on them by other people (both male and female).

This informs our understanding of certain ideas or behaviours that can be permitted expression in some intersubjective space and others which the subject feels must be hidden. In my previous research with male prisoners (Evans and Wallace 2008), participants expressed this concept brilliantly as 'things that must be kept off the landing' (p.5) (i.e. away from the gaze or policing of other men). The research interview, or even more the therapeutic relationship, may become a space where it is safe to let this mask slip in the presence of another. Crossley (1996) believes that we learn 'intersubjective scripts concerning the appropriateness of certain types of action to certain types of situation and that we develop "back regions" in which to let the mask slip' (p.47). Masculinity is often achieved by rigorously avoiding displaying anything associated with femininity and homosexuality. Saussure (cited in Danaher *et al.* 2000) outlines the way structuralist thinking sees this issue by arguing that all meaning is relational. In other words, to understand what the word 'man' means you have to relate it to other concepts which it is not: woman, child, girl or boy.

> ### Reflection Point
>
> **DIALOGUE**
>
> - Which ideas, thoughts and feelings do you tend to keep out of relational space and its associated dialogue?
> - What happens to you if there are very limited spaces in which you can speak the darker parts of your inner world?
> - With whom do you regularly dialogue about the deeper aspects of you? What is it about the relational dynamic with that person that makes you feel safe enough to talk this way?

Martin Buber's I–Thou

'All real life is meeting' – this famous quote from Martin Buber's classic work, *I and Thou,* Buber (1923, p.25) distinguishes between the 'I–Thou' relationship that is direct, mutual, present, open, and the 'I-It'– relation in which one relates to the other only indirectly and non-mutually, both knowing and using the other...

> I am called into being by you and you by me. When you embrace me as the unique person that I am and when you confront me in your own uniqueness, we confirm each other... as the unique persons we are called to become...I meet you from my ground and you meet me from yours, and our lives interpenetrate as person meeting person in the life of dialogue. Our very sense of ourselves comes only in our meeting with others as they confirm us in the life of dialogue. (Buber 1923, p.72)

This is a shared gift we give each other: we welcome the other in their real otherness to us, even as they welcome us in our real otherness to them. In this way, both Self and Other are always co-established. Thus both the distance of difference and the closeness of relatedness exist at one and the same time.

The Streams in the Consulting Room

DIALOGUE

You may be opening your client to types and patterns of dialoguing that they have not shared with many people before. As therapists we need to create the permission, and model ways of dialoguing, that allow people to open to different forms of talking and meeting.

It means we need to be very alert to the client's ways of talking with us, their self-talk and the types of dialogue they have with key attachment figures in the present and during their childhood.

Dominant forms of discourse shape the self, the subject positions the person adopts in power systems and affect how much control they feel they have over themselves and their future life.

Maladaptive discourses that have been habitual and become unconscious may be a vital element of the change work.

I–Thou is not dualistic separation, nor is it fused oneness. It is real meeting, with all its attendant freedom, open-endedness and unexpectedness. Being 'confirmed by the other' is not the same, at all, as that socialisation which forces us to comply or fit in, and creates the split between False Self and True Self. When the intersubjective realm offers not real relationship but just a pre-existent order that we must take our identity from, then I–Thou is lost. I–Thou is a meeting of two different 'personal cores', in which each core goes out of itself to be with, to participate in, to interpenetrate, the other core.

The Key to DIALOGUE is to remember that it's not a monologue – be as keen to hear what they have to say as you are to formulate what you might say next.

STREAM 10: SPACE AND PLACE

Let there be spaces in your togetherness…
Give your hearts, but not into each other's keeping.
For only the hand of Life can contain your hearts.
And stand together yet not too near together:
For the pillars of the temple stand apart,
And the oak tree and the cypress grow not in each other's shadow.

Kahlil Gibran (1991, p.16)

Relationships take place within spaces. We live in space, and through social-spatial relations within spaces our identities are formed and we come to know ourselves as distinct from others, and in connection with and in separation from others. We are embraced by space, we are inhabited by space and we inhabit space. Conceptualising space can draw from sociology, psychology, architecture, social epidemiology, social psychiatry and neuroscience, and from the arts, from dance, theatre, literature, poetry or painting.

All disciplines, in sciences or arts, and all counselling models, like people, derive and seek shape and definition by the spaces, the grounds, the place they seek and negotiate occupancy of. Epistemology itself can be considered from a spatial perspective as a concern with the limits and boundaries of knowledge.

Conceptualising space here draws from arguments of the of 'mind–body dualism'. Our emotional and psychological well-being is situated within the spaces of our 'natural' and 'built' physical and social landscapes. In a dynamic continuous dialogue we move in and through space creating symbolic and imagined spaces and dreamscapes. We live in and through 'places' within space, of complex personal, cultural and spiritual significance. We look out from one space into another, our 'being in the world' is a location in space, a place we have occupancy of. We perceive and conceptualise from the physical location of where we are, seeing to the right or left, looking above or below, near or far. Each perspective is a view taken from and in relation to the place we are in. Husserl talks of the 'nullpoint' in the experience of the body in space; the lived body, even in the midst of motion, is 'here' where we are located, the absolute 'here' of situated experience from which all 'theres' are perceived. We look 'forward' to things happening, we look 'back' at the past; we do both in the present from the place we are in. Therapeutic space is a contested space with its own specific complexities.

The Streams in the Consulting Room

SPACE AND PLACE

The reason we think about the setting in therapy is because the psychological is very affected by the physical space we are in. This is why different models have strong views on how the therapy room should be: from the blank, minimalist psychoanalytic space (possibly alienating?) to the warm, welcoming person-centred space (possibly infantilising?).

If you are lucky enough to have control over the physical space where you work with clients when is the last time you really stopped to think about the messages it is giving? Is it full of books, certificates, art, colour, what sorts of furniture, photographs – how do you imagine different types of clients might experience this space and your presence in it?

Therapeutic space is the interpersonal space between people, between the counsellor and the client, and the intrapersonal space within, crossing feelings, thoughts and memories of the persons involved there. The identity of therapeutic space itself, once, arguably, fundamentally defined by psychological and psychotherapeutic theories of relationship, the space of Winnicott's 'respite and containment', has in recent years been increasingly defined as a space of wider political and economic demands for accountability, assessments and evidence. So therapeutic space takes its 'place' within broader geographic, cultural and political landscapes, all of which are spaces and all of which are heavily invested in by human action. Such human actions, from a situated perspective, are a potential presence in every therapeutic space and in each counselling session.

Space exists between people; it defines individual and collective identity, and challenges it. Space provides for the Me, and I, and the You and Other, and the space 'inbetween' allows for congruence, empathy and the 'Place' of Buber's I and Thou, mentioned in the Dialogue stream. Space is here, between this page and you the reader. It's here between each character in this typeface, shaping and giving form, offering aesthetic experience from the space each character occupies and is defined by. From its depths, shapes and profile, it occupies space within our thoughts. Here, now, in this space, between you and the page, and internally between your perception and reflection, within you, these images and words suggest and neurologically create, between synapse and synapse, thinking space as you consider and interpret their meanings. From the perspective of situated practice, space is rich in meanings, a weave of images, emotions and symbols. Space, once acted in, becomes place, becomes a place of relationships. Relationships define physical spaces, and spaces shift and are reshaped by relationships.

Consider one of the most fundamental of human requirements, a home. An investment transforms a space with a physical building that becomes a house, a house becomes a home. Once human agency is involved in space, it is no longer inert. In this instance it is no longer defined by its investment, or its external presentation, or by photographs and images in the estate agents. As 'home' space it is now in continuous transition, transition initiated by relationships of differing kinds, all dynamic and evolving. 'Home' has no single meaning. The space of 'Home' as a lived experience defies generalisation. Home can be both a container of projections and a reflection of whose home it is, a place of dynamic interplay. This example of space in transition may serve as a narrative of how the situated perspective can suggest, unearth, the narrative, the living story within even the most physical of spaces. Ask a builder where architects' plans (the model) and the builder's experience (the situated experience) meet up and where they depart from one another. In that conversation will be another story of the relationships between models and practice – where they meet in a space and where they may separate.

> ### Reflection Point
>
> **SPACE AND PLACE**
>
> - *Think about three places that you have deep attachments to. What do they mean to you? What feelings emerge when you imagine them?*
> - *Think about a space where you have felt unwelcome, unseen or unsafe – why do you think it felt that way?*
> - *Now imagine a space where you felt you belonged, were welcome, understood, relaxed – in what ways was it different from the unsafe space above?*
> - *What happens to your body, mind, emotions and behaviours when you are in these two different spaces?*

Give yourself some space and some time in that space to consider the relationship between Space and Place. Consider now what space is offered to you by being asked to 'read this', in contrast to what might be involved in 'dwelling with this'. Consider then this view of Place from the art historian and feminist writer, Lucy Lippard:

> Place is latitudinal and longitudinal within the map of a person's life. It is temporal and spatial, personal and political. A layered location replete with human histories and memories, place has width as well as depth. It is about connections, what surrounds it, what formed it, what happened there, what will happen there. (1997, p.7)

Consider this stream as one you are entirely immersed in – even now by reading and paying attention to this particular textual space. As you engage in the flux of sense making, negotiating across the external space of this paper and the internal space of feelings, thoughts and experiences you may find yourself blurring the boundaries between intrapersonal space of thought and reflexivity and the interpersonal space of the writer and reader.

Full too, is the therapeutic or counselling space of situated practice, for from the perspective of situated practice, the place of the meeting between counsellor and client constitutes a therapeutic landscape, a landscape of physical, social and symbolic and temporal spaces. Spatially, the social space of the therapeutic meeting, shapes, manages, defines, organises and influences what takes place there. The therapeutic space is a product of human action, a place of contested dialogues, of human actions that create, and produce experience, history, knowledge and consciousness. The therapeutic landscape is a space defined by physical dimensions and overlaid with human presence and culture. As a product of social action it is rich in symbolic meanings and richly detailed with the aesthetics of the therapeutic encounter. Is the therapy space the therapeutic space when it's empty, or only when it's occupied? Do the projections and poetics of the counsellor and the clients, in their physical absence, still occupy the space?

Generally we meet only the surface space of things. But all spaces echo with depths that await being attended to, listened to, heard from within, and discovered by situated practice.

 The Key to SPACE AND PLACE is empathy (being able to consider how another will experience a space very familiar to you) and awareness (thinking about possible interpretations of the things you choose to put into – or leave out of – the space in which you practice).

CHAPTER 3
DIVING DEEPER

- Seeing, Listening, Feeling
- Embodiment
- Immersion
- Intuition
- Empathy
- Tacit knowledge
- Humour
- Warmth

In many ways this set of streams is the core toolkit we need with us on our journey to mastery. We sometimes call them the 'avenues of immersion', ways of allowing ourselves to delve ever deeper and more completely into the terrain. When applied to working with clients in therapy they are vital skills to bring with you each time you sit down in the therapist's chair. This set of streams enables us to delve deeper once we have been able to enter the space and dialogue, the play and exploration, opened up the stories and metaphors encountered in the 'Jumping In' chapter. It is worth repeating here that it would be ridiculous to try to follow these streams in some sort of sequential order – that would be totally contrary to the spirit of situated practice. We weave with multiple strands of thread simultaneously once our feet touch down in real-world territory (as the later stream Juggling explores) or as our head goes beneath the waves and we allow ourselves to get wet.

However, it is useful to conceptualise this group together as they all focus on getting under the skin, beneath the surface and entering into the core of another person's heart and mind – employing as much situated skill as we own to get inside this person's way of being in the world and seeing the world.

STREAM 11: SEEING, LISTENING, FEELING

Seeing with the eyes of another, listening with the ears of another, and feeling with the heart of another.

Alfred Adler

In our reflective practice work at university we begin by asking our students to explore what we call the 'avenues of immersion'. These are ways in which the therapist can become fully immersed in the intersubjective space between themselves and their client. The avenues allow us to get inside the internal world of the person we are working with, trying to experience the world from their perspective. These tasks represent the root of all empathy: and for the client, in feeling your attempts to be with them and understand their world, the seeds of trust, feeling heard and contained, can be planted. The three key ways of immersing ourselves are seeing, listening and feeling.

I have placed this stream first in the 'Diving Deeper' chapter as the six streams that follow: embodiment, immersion, intuition, empathy, tacit knowledge, humour and warmth are tributaries of this stream. It is hard to use humour sensitively and appropriately or to feel *genuine* warmth if we have not really entered this person's world. I would argue that empathy, immersion and intuition are severely hampered in practice if we haven't opened up our channels of seeing, listening and feeling.

Our students often ask: in what way are these streams different from the seeing, listening and feeling we do in everyday life? This turns out to be the very best question.

Much of our visual system as humans is shared with all animals (even worms) – it allows us to react to light and to take in and process visual information from our environment. The lens in the eye focuses an image onto the retina, which converts patterns of light into neuronal signals to send to the brain's central ganglia. It's a fascinating process and one which is fairly mechanical. Far more interesting from the lived experience viewpoint is what we end up focusing on and its emotional impact on us. The vast majority of visual information is only selectively attended to, yet if we see our child's face looking sad or richly coloured flowers or a traffic accident our attention is gripped. I can still form the visual image in my mind's eye of watching the sun rise over the Grand Canyon, or the smile on the face of the first person I fell in love with – some imagery sticks around. More distressing imagery we tend to block out: a shard of glass sticking out of my arm during bar work 20 years ago, photographs of bodies following post-mortems when I worked in the law courts – for some people the sight of a father beating a mother, seeing a partner acting sexually with someone else yet unaware of your presence, the vision of a wife during the end stages of breast cancer.

Years ago a firefighter I was working with said, 'When a building is on fire most people run away; we have to run towards.' For therapists it is similar, although not as physically dangerous. We must look deeply into people's anger, pain, loneliness, existential terror, grief or self-loathing without flinching or turning away yet without becoming so hard and immune that we cannot be deeply moved any more.

> ### The Streams in the Consulting Room
>
> **SEEING, LISTENING, FEELING**
> To be truly open to these avenues of immersion – you have to get out of the way. Your ego, fears, narcissistic tendencies, needing to be liked or be clever, your hunger, the lingering anger from the row with your partner last night – all have to give way (temporarily) to the journey into this other person's unique inner world.
>
> This involves effort and some sacrifice – yet it is also wonderful. The chance to flee the bonds of self-hood (and all its associated trials and heaviness) for a while is marvellously freeing. At times when life has been truly awful therapy space has acted as a small holiday from personal pain and has re-opened me to the world outside of self.

Our everyday version of seeing: half paying attention to thousands of competing images, and jumping to rapid, judgemental conclusions about what we see, will not work well in therapy space. That trait (of rushing to quick judgement) is necessary for animals to survive in the wild (or for humans in modern settings). Stopping to contemplate the internal motivation of that tiger hurtling towards you is hardly a sensible survival strategy. The trouble is that the automatic process of uber-fast decision making hampers us if we wish to build intimacy and increase trust – it can become problematic in the context of relationship making. Part of the reason for Slowing Down is to gradually allow things to take form, to revise first impressions and to really pay attention to detail. Seeing into (or in-sight) is the polar opposite of stereotyping (putting things into neat categories or boxes) or prejudice (pre-judgement). It is attempting to freshly encounter things as they actually are – which lies at the heart of phenomenology.

Listening is much the same: we tend to say 'I hear you' or 'I get what you're saying' when half the time we are merely trying to rush in with what we have to say next. We angrily shout 'Listen' at someone who we feel is not really open to our side of the story. In childhood this is common: children to be seen and not heard. Good parents are genuinely willing and able to listen to their child (at least sometimes!) but sadly many parents cannot or will not hear what their child is really feeling. Some of us know the pain of rarely feeling able to voice our true feelings growing up – it may have been dangerous to do so, perhaps the people in our family were poor at managing real feelings and didn't model it for us or maybe we had felt mocked, teased or shamed for being too sensitive, too clever, not clever enough, too different, not different enough and so on. There are so many settings in which the voice of the real self learns to hide as we grow: interactions with parents, siblings, friends, school and places of worship. We internalise the social rules around politeness, appropriateness and good manners so that we don't 'show ourselves up' or 'let anyone else down'. We need to belong and fit in – to feel wanted – so we learn to be good little hypocrites just like the rest of the herd. Some of this is necessary – it is part of emotional self-regulation to know when to express something appropriately, to learn delayed gratification and self-discipline, to consider others' feelings – so we do not become too selfish or psychopathic, yet too often the shutting down of the real voice goes too far and begins to really hurt us.

Reflection Point

SEEING, LISTENING, FEELING

- Spend five minutes staring closely at something familiar: the back of your hand, a tree, your front door. What do you notice when you pay close attention? How is this different from your normal experience of this everyday object?

- Listen to a song that is not sung in a language you know – if this person had a story what would it be? What are they feeling? Try to hear the voice of the heart.

- Feeling: the next time you feel 'upset', 'out of sorts' or 'bored' – try to tune in to the deeper feelings underlying these ordinary states.

It works the other way too. If we are honest with ourselves much of the time when we claim to be listening to others a good part of us is still caught up with our own needs, sensations and worries. We all do it and pretend we aren't. Naturally we know when someone's attention is only partly with us – we can feel it. Usually we take turns and switch the conversation back to them if we fear we are boring them – even whilst we are feeling sulky and resentful at having to do so. In therapy space we must work hard not to play these games too much – the space between us in here must feel different from the space between people out there, if it is to become a place in which psychological healing can occur. Attention to this is vital – which is why Space and Place is one of the streams.

There is a simple and profound power in somebody truly listening to how we feel. Not to the words particularly, the sentence structure, grammar or vocabulary – rather to the emotional content, what we have come to call the *music under the words*, which is really the voice of the heart. This is what the therapist must try to hear. It may be a tune that the client barely knows themselves, one which even their loved ones struggle to fully know, or may be unable to listen to, but if the client really feels you have heard it (and felt its inbuilt emotion on your pulse as on their own) something transformational may begin. Initially the words used by clients may mask the real song – we all feel pressure to be liked, to seem happier than we really are, perhaps not to impose too much on the good will of others. They may be terrified of the real song, ashamed or angered by it, maybe the music has been in their life for so long they can hardly pick out the melody anymore; yet this secret song of the heart may form the centre of what pains them, keeps them stuck in life or may speak of the real self who is longing for release. Even if nobody else can hear it, as therapists we must try.

Deeply connected to seeing and listening is feeling. Therapists need to have good self-regulation (the ability to manage our cognitive, emotional and behavioural responses to the environment) to stay with appropriate and holding reactions which are empathically attuned to the client and their needs even when we may be feeling lost, preoccupied or overwhelmed ourselves. We also need to be aware of feelings as they are among our best tools for understanding what is going on for the client. When we are experiencing a flood of countertransference response to a grieving client we must tease apart our own memories, past griefs and unconscious reactions from the client's. This can never be exact science, but openness to our own feeling state and the capacity to evaluate and reflect on it is tied to good practice. In therapy the feelings we have are triggered by what we see and hear: the catch in the voice, the rueful smile, the glistening eye that speaks of unshed tears, the tension in the body when talking about childhood pain. I have often used the question 'if your tears could speak what would they say?' to a client consumed with crying and struggling to verbalise their emotions. Silences, tears, resentment, fear – all have their own energy, beyond that which is audible or visible, that we can tune into if we are fully present and engaged.

 The Key to SEEING, LISTENING, FEELING is developing a practised sensitivity to what is outside you and what you experience within you – and letting go of the rush to judgement which the world forces us into.

STREAM 12: EMBODIMENT

There is more wisdom in your body than in your deepest philosophy.

Friedrich Nietzche (1969)

It is through our senses that we receive information from the external world of others and the internal world of ourselves. We may elect to block, defend or absorb that information. Our responses, our learning in and from any situation are a process of perception, attention, concentration and intention. By this means we create patterns of interaction within and without ourselves that configure our experiences of the world. The embodied counsellor consciously works within the interrelationship of the different senses as they are involved in the patterning and weaving of engagement in the living world. Embodiment, in the meaning intended here, is the recognition of the primacy of the counsellor's body in relationship to others, and to the environment, as the hub of interpersonal experience and individual and collective sense making, and as a primary characteristic of situated practice. Such a position is in contrast to, for example, approaches in which it is the intellectual or theoretical constructs of the counsellor that serve as the foremost source of informing and validating the process of the therapeutic encounter.

The Streams in the Consulting Room

EMBODIMENT

Two of the best sources of information in the therapy room are what the client's body is doing and how your own body is feeling.

Particularly with the clients who experienced trauma in childhood, or learned to disassociate as a form of protection, helping them to recognise the body memory which arises when they are working through strong emotions can be really beneficial.

Noting my own body's reactions to material assists me in identifying countertransference, projective identification and deepening my empathic attunement. If I listen well it also assists me in recognising intuitive flashes.

The embodied experience may be developed and explored through a focus on the sensorium of the counsellor which can be best understood as the crucible made up of the sensory, psychological and phenomenal perceptions of the counsellor. Our senses offer five distinct sources of knowledge and experience and in turn structure our relationship with the world. The dominance of any one sense over the others in turn determines and constrains experience and learning. It is argued that in the twenty-first century the world of media technology, written text and externally produced imagery have taken on the role as the dominant source of individual sense making, replacing smell which until relatively recent times played a much more significant role as a source of knowledge. Sight, so closely associated with the brain and mental reasoning, can contribute to a particular isolation from the range of situated knowledge available to the human sensorium. The packaged fruit and meat of the supermarket appeals primarily to the visual sense, to the cognitive, revealing little of the quality or pleasure to the primary senses of taste and smell associated with the consumption of food. This loss of initial direct embodied contact and sense making with our food is now textually, symbolically represented as computer-generated 'display' and 'use by' dates in much of the developed world's retail industry.

> ### Reflection Point
>
> **EMBODIMENT**
>
> - How do you typically experience emotional pain in your body? Where does it show up?
> - Recall a memory of experiencing emotional comfort from someone else as a child – how is your body involved in this memory?
> - Think about how the following emotions impact you physically: shame, loneliness, anger, yearning, guilt.

Sensory knowledge is often ineffable, often outside of verbal reasoning, but is nevertheless experienced, real, impressing, and an inherent part of any life situation. Our senses have an independence from our conscious control and play active independent roles delivering silent knowledge and understanding that often lies hidden from our consciousness of the human condition in our daily engagement with the lived world we inhabit.

Sensory and embodied experience sits at the heart of situated practice and the engagement with the client. The intersubjectivity of the relationship between counsellor and client may blur and soften the boundary between self and the world in the co-transferences of the therapeutic relationship. Embodied situated practice asks that the counsellor focus on their sensory, body awareness at the same time as focusing on, for example, the language of the client, the shared external space and the shared inner mental space. The situated practice of the counsellor supports the creation of the therapeutic potential in the safe, facilitative space of the counselling room. Such a counselling space is potent with embodied experience for the counsellor, evoking in their senses the beingness of a situated counsellor in action. The beingness of the counsellor may be said to be redefined, recontoured within this therapeutic landscape, a felt landscape formed and wounded by the acts of man.

The languaging of the body's experience is often problematic and challenging to the received ideas about language. Describing the experience of embodied language and into the felt, intuitive uncertain space of the emergent, sometimes conflicting aspects of one's own feelings and that of our clients.

Reflecting and writing on reflections are important elements of this module. Embodied writing invites you to bring the finely textured weave of human experience into words, to evoke, from within, words and senses from the sensuous living world, to sometimes take creative risks in order to evoke for the reader, and oneself representations in writing that resonate with the visceral counselling encounter of attunement, resonance and sensation. To perhaps explore reflective poetic forms of writing, that seek to bring forth, in a multisensory representation, the embodied encounter of the situated student practitioner.

 The Key to EMBODIMENT is paying attention to what the body is doing and feeling – particularly when the body is expressing something different from the mouth or the face.

STREAM 13: IMMERSION

The moment of truth, the sudden emergence of a new insight, is an act of intuition. Such intuitions give the appearance of miraculous flushes; or short-circuits of reasoning. In fact they may be likened to an immersed chain, of which only the beginning and the end are visible above the surface of consciousness. The driver vanishes at one end of the chain and comes up at the other end, guided by invisible links.

Arthur Koestler (1989)

Imagine a young child sitting nervously on the side of a swimming pool. They have been watching other people swim for a while now and have been given some instruction in water safety. Mum and Dad and several friends have tried to explain what it feels like to be in the water. All of this helps to prepare them for the next step. However, these pictures painted by others are inadequate, they can never fully communicate what that first rush of water over the head feels like. We cannot properly explain an experience to someone. It always falls short. In order to have the experience they must jump in the pool, not sit on the edge talking about it.

To really begin to know new terrain we must *immerse* ourselves in it. We must jump in, get wet, go under the surface, and relinquish control. This stream is deeply connected to Stream 1: The Leap of Faith – in that it takes courage and a willingness to let go. The difference is that the leap is concerned with the run-up to jumping off the cliff – whilst immersion is about what you learn once you hit the water. The metaphor of jumping in to a pool is apt here – your head must go under, you are likely to feel overwhelmed at first. In new territory we must get wet in order to begin to know it well. If you have ever watched somebody swim who is terrified of getting their face or hair wet you will know what I mean – you must relinquish some control and allow yourself to be affected by this new territory. The rigidly models-led mindset tries not to get its hair wet, to stay above and separated from this new world, to not be changed by it. In really tasting the situated world we cannot do this.

Therapist as diving teacher

Part of immersion is feeling comfortable going under the surface: into the unconscious, the half-forgotten, the shadow, the split-off trauma, the denied existential angst, body memory and the hated, fear-inducing parts of the self. If we are to serve as a safe pair of hands for the client to make such treacherous, but necessary, journeys we must be used to these places ourselves – both within the self and within the psyche of others. It needs practice – which is why most of us explore ourselves in therapy during our training and why we get our students to engage in reflective and challenging experiential work right from the start of their degrees. Much of humanity is not at ease under the psychological surface – they will engage in any number of defensive manoeuvres to stay away from such murky depths. The media and the pace of modern living all tend to focus on the surface of things, the cultural spotlight moves and spins rapidly from celebrity to product to movie to YouTube viral video. As Bret Easton Ellis says in his novel *Glamorama* (1998, p.112), 'we slide down the surface of things'.

The wise therapist must be different and learn to become skilled at helping others navigate the deeper currents – that is where most human pain is formed and where genuine healing takes place. Living at top-speed superficial level is hurting many people's psyche in the modern urban world – therapy space must be different, acting as an antidote to the sometimes impersonal, uncaring, crowded, techno-drenched world outside.

> ### Reflection Point
>
> **IMMERSION**
>
> - *Recall how you were feeling the first time you ever went for some form of professional help – what feelings, thoughts, fears and fantasies predominated?*
> - *Or when you have had to share a secret with a friend or loved one?*
> - *Immersion is about encountering new territory and allowing ourselves to encounter its depths – is there an area of your life right now where you are clinging to the edge of the pool and finding it hard to let go?*
> - *What will it take for you to go under the surface?*

Cognitive immersion helps you to learn

This immersion is one of the major foundations in situatedness.

This has to do with transitions, defences and resistances: the processes involved in letting go of a more models-led mode of learning and function, and embracing a more situated one. Thus: what is this transition, and might it involve a stage of being all at sea, bereft of the old but not yet sure of the new? What are the blocks to even making such a transition? Why might some people make it easier than others? Why might some people resist situatedness *en bloc*, whilst others resist only pieces of it? Is the challenge to embracing situatedness more of a personal nature, or more to do with 'getting' its logic and strategy? Might there be any discernible order to the steps by which a person switches from reliance on models to situatedness?

The learning journey has to do with noteworthy learning events, and the way they weave together to produce alterations in understanding and skill. Thus: what is the discovery process that occurs in the situation? Does it have any discernible structure, or logic? What is it like to undergo its ups and downs, ins and outs, or its refusal to let us know all we might need to know in advance? Why might mistakes and failures be as vital to this learning process as successes? How do key learning events make a coherent whole over time?

> ### The Streams in the Consulting Room
>
> **IMMERSION**
>
> The more experienced you are as a practitioner the more you should have learned to immerse yourself – but there are always deeper levels to which we can travel. Challenging ourselves to push further down is what separates a good therapist from a truly wise one.
>
> Most of the time, however, immersion shows up in the room when we must work with nervous swimmers, needing to dive deeply into the self – but scared to let go of the side of the pool and go under the water.
>
> We should never forget how it felt for us the first few times we did this and strive to offer strong encouragement and support yet never force people before they are ready.

In the Reflective Practice module and all of the skills training and experiential work on our two degrees (Psychology & Counselling and Therapeutic Psychology) we explicitly give permission and create space for students to struggle with the situated action mode – and it is usually something of a struggle at first due to its clash with the educative/learning context that is more usually academic, and which students have been trained in at primary school, secondary school and college. Struggle is inbuilt to situatedness (it is one of the later streams) and we encourage our students to be more concerned with the Travelling and the Fight along the Way, rather than with any particular outcome. You get to try situatedness out for yourselves, reflect on its operation and potential importance for therapy. The broad aim is to enlarge the sphere of reflection by bringing in new data. The end result is new information, insight and evaluation. The difference is that the data are not theories, experiments, statistical tests, but the outcomes of experience and practice.

When we neglect our experiences we skim over them, stay fairly uninvolved and are only partly present. This can create a bias toward quick responding, which seems more like a sort of bloodless 'in and out'. This can generate insight, like fire crackers fizzing through the air, but not understanding. Understanding takes much longer to crystallise, and only develops if we are really 'submerged' in the situation. It is necessary to get 'down into it', 'get our hands dirty' rather than remaining 'high and dry'.

Accepting experience is tantamount to accepting true immersion. This is why presence *to*, immersion *in*, and relationship *with*, the terrain is so important.

The dynamic here is less like riding the wave, and more like being thrown into the water 'at the deep end'. This is why no amount of teaching how to swim through diagrams on a blackboard, or even mimicking the movements required, will help the non-swimmer. They just have to experience being in water. This applies to everything on the ground. Until we have 'experienced it', we just do not know what it is, in the truth it brings to us. That truth is a music that is not simply externally heard, but plays on the drum of the heart, making it beat in a certain way. One reason most adults are tempted to run from such learning is that it has become suffused with fear, expectation and the terror of getting it wrong. Young children do not naturally learn in this way, their curiosity knows no bounds. They do not need to know where the next step in the journey is taking them; instead they delight in the twists and turns and can easily become so absorbed that all sense of time and self – and worry – is gone. For the situated practitioner, recapturing something of that childhood ability is crucial.

 The Key to IMMERSION is courage – being willing to lose your head for a while and go under the waves – it is only then you can begin to develop true confidence in the deep waters of the human psyche.

STREAM 14: INTUITION

> Albert Einstein called the intuitive or metaphoric mind a sacred gift. He added that the rational mind was a faithful servant. It is paradoxical that in the context of modern life we have begun to worship the servant and defile the devine.
>
> Matthew Stein (2000, p.26)

The idea behind Einstein's gift is that intuitive mind is sacred, hard-won and increasingly disrespected in the speed of the modern world. We must practice so it can develop. Practice makes perfect, but the wrong kind of practice gets you into bad habits. This is just as true for the practice of music, sport, dance, DJing, judo, acting as it is for psychotherapy and counselling. In reality we don't reproduce in any mechanical way or imitative way what we have practised in exercises. Somehow various things are woven together in the here and now of the living situation that cannot be done outside of it. You can think of it as 'being in the zone' – not just the mind thinking about it, but the body, the heart and the soul being there too. This is deeply connected to the experiences of trance and flow which we will explore in more depth later. The well is not a machine: it is affected by emotion, situation – some days you cannot draw water, other days the water is polluted and on yet others the bucket gets stuck and just won't rise to the surface. Yet we know there are some things you can do to help kick start it. For example, it is much easier to get into the well in dialogue, in performance, being witnessed by an audience.

The weaving together cannot be mapped in advance of it actually happening. It therefore always has some spontaneity and improvisation in it, an element of creation *in situ*. There is an element of inspiration and magic. If you sit in fear not knowing which way to go nothing will come to you, but if you start walking regardless of the fear the universe (or the well) will move towards you and assist.

The truth is that sometimes we are more able to access our intuitive mind than others – usually on days when we are able to get out of our own way. The conscious mind does not drive intuition – it is too slow. If we rely on the conscious mind too much what seems to be intuitive might very well be something else – prejudice, pre-existing beliefs, bits of theory, personal preferences masquerading as intuition. The real thing tends to come up from the unconscious mind, the body, the emotional self, the energetic field between you and your client – from an intangible place that moves faster than the mechanical brain can handle. It frequently shows up as fragments of feeling, imagery, like a door just waiting to be gently pushed open – rather than anything concrete and ready formed.

It feels rather more like the remnants of dreams – sand slipping through fingers, flickering embers, sparks in the sky – than solid blocks of wood. Perhaps this is why we find it harder to trust it when we are sitting in the professional role of therapeutic practitioner. We put pressure on ourselves to know for sure what we are doing and follow the rules, particularly when we are new to the field. Requiring absolute certainty when working with another emotional, complex, messy human being will only disable the intuitive flow and trap us into mistrusting it when it shows up.

Reflection Point

INTUITION

- *Think of a time when an intuitive feeling turned out to be correct. Now think of an occasion when an intuitive feeling turned out to be wrong.*
- *Reflecting on these, can you identify any differences in how these two 'intuitive moments' presented themselves to you?*
- *As a child what messages were you given around being an intuitive person, particularly from members of your own gender?*
- *As a practitioner what messages does your profession give you about intuition?*

Acting on an intuitive flash whilst working must always be tentative – we can never really be quite sure where the intuitive feeling is coming from and whether it will feel right for the client – so it must be offered or shared gently at first to see if it resonates with them. What I have learned over the years is that when these intuitive flashes come they provide fantastic shortcut moments if they are shared in the right way. Often, for me, they come as pictures in my head, or tensions in my body, as metaphors from film, TV or books that when brought into the room turn out to capture excellently something that was 'floating in the air' or 'bubbling just under the surface' in the room.

As a male practitioner I have worked to build this into my practice. Boys are usually taught that intuition is the province of women – who ever heard of *a man's intuition* – and may feel that this is not something they have a natural affinity for. And women may feel that any reliance on intuition may risk stripping away their hard-won sense of professionalism – that they may be mocked or derided for it. Certainly during training both genders are likely to feel cautious about saying that any aspect of the therapy comes from an intuitive place rather than theory or evidence-based research. Supervisors can assist here by owning this element of their own practice and encouraging trainees to explore and reflect upon moments of intuition during therapy.

The Streams in the Consulting Room

INTUITION

With clients who find it hard to feel or describe their emotions you may find much charged emotional energy is left circulating in the room and your intuitive side may pick this up.

Paying close attention to this is a really powerful way of understanding what it feels like being this person and gives you a unique entrance key into the treasure house of their heart and their buried psyche.

Fortunately there is a growing body of work which is fleshing out the idea of intuition having a central place in psychotherapeutic practice based on our understanding of neuroscience. Terry Marks-Tarlow (2012) in her ground-breaking book *Clinical Intuition in Psychotherapy* acknowledges this longstanding 'problem' with intuition: that it can seem like 'magic' or 'mysticism' to those watching or even to those experiencing it. Psychology has more than a century of history of trying to prove itself a *proper science* and the hangover of this need has been felt all the way from Freud and his 'Project for a Scientific Psychology' (1977 [1895]) in the 1890s through to today's reification of evidence-based CBT practice. Against such pressure the embracing of intuition as a valid instrument for the professional therapist has faced major obstacles – the therapy tool that dare not speak its name in serious company. Marks-Tarlow's work argues that 'clinical intuition fills the gap between theory and practice... accentuates perception of relational patterns in self and others...and is a necessary ingredient for deep change in psychotherapy' (p.3). Clearly this fits in precisely with what I am putting forward as the situated action position.

Allan Schore (2012) supports this notion and maintains that we can properly understand clinical intuition as the operation, at speed and unconsciously, of non-verbal, right-brain to right-brain communication and empathic attunement occurring within the therapeutic dyad. Whilst its operation may be very rapid, the gradual cultivation of our intuitive self that fills the well requires us to slow down and pay attention, to listen, to feel – which is very closely related to the Seeing, Listening, Feeling stream discussed earlier in this chapter. Intuition comes up from the depths – it doesn't thrive on the surface and your ability to trust that it has useful information for you will only be consolidated when you have dared to bring it into the interpersonal field.

 The Key to INTUITION is to listen for the flashes of intuition and practise trusting it.

STREAM 15: EMPATHY

Could a greater miracle take place than for us to look through each other's eyes for an instant?

Henry David Thoreau

If each new client in therapy is a fresh piece of terrain we must spend time getting to know the lie of the land, how things look from their vantage point. What does the world look like through their eyes? Our greatest tool for doing this lies in the use of empathy.

Rollo May, in his classic work *The Art of Counselling* (1965) asks: How does one personality meet and react to another? At some level it is by each making an attempt to understand and feel the emotional and psychological world of the other. Empathy is a translation of a word used by German psychologists '*einfulung*' – feeling into. It is derived from the Greek '*pathos*' meaning a deep and strong feeling akin to suffering. May described it as 'a much deeper state of identification of personalities in which one person so feels in to the other as temporarily to lose his or her identity' (May 1965, p.61). It is in this space that understanding, compassion, communication and influence can take place.

The Challenge of Empathy

Empathy is work. It is not surface-level sympathy which is easily given and dipped in sugary condescension. It is easy to empathise with someone whose experiences are judged 'victimless' or whose life experience is close to your own. It is much harder to extend your empathic attunement to people whose experiences, motivations and behaviour may be condemned or judged and may be very different to your own beliefs. It takes more discipline and courage to stay connected to the internal world of someone whose wavelength is unfamiliar, which may disturb, challenge or upset you.

This is where morality must be applied in a way different from that commonly understood. As therapists, when we agree to travel with someone into their psychological territory we do not go as a moral judge or jury, rather as a guide, a support, a fellow traveller. To that end we must learn to separate the person from the behaviour, if the behaviour is something with which we personally disagree. Even if our internal terrain is dramatically different from that of the client we can allow ourselves to connect to the underlying feelings of their experience.

We have all felt sadness, loss, love, shame, rage, joy, disappointment, success or loneliness – even though it may have been in very different contexts.

Communicating your empathic attunement to the client may be one of the most therapeutic things you can do. Yet, Kohut (1981) also understood that empathy could only be relevant to human interaction if it results in a response that follows directly from one's experience-near observations (things we notice either during or very soon after the expereience itself), which Kohut sees as linking empathy and action while emphasising their differences: by this he means that it is only when one is able to step into another's shoes, to see the world through the other's eyes that one is able to generate an authentic, accurate, fitting response. The use of empathy in the clinical setting is partly for the purpose of understanding and explaining what one has observed but is primarily for the purpose of communicating our understanding back to the client so that they can internalise this. This is a perfect fit with our philosophy of reflective practice and thinking about action after it takes place.

> ### Reflection Point
>
> **EMPATHY**
>
> - *How does it feel when you are in relationship with someone who struggles with being empathically attuned to your internal world?*
> - *What, for you, is the difference between empathy and sympathy?*
> - *What are your personal blocks when you try to 'feel into' another person's emotional inner world?*

The Failures of Empathy

We can never get it right every time. Whether as therapists, parents, drivers or cooks we often make mistakes. It is impossible to be perfectly empathically attuned all the time as therapists (it is just the same for parents). In fact we wouldn't want to be. Heinz Kohut taught us that such failures are of great value to clients: they are what make *transmuting internalisations* possible, whereby the self-soothing internal structures of the client get a chance to build. From a psychodynamic viewpoint empathy is analogous to the capacity to identify a face in a single act of perception. It is one of the earliest skills we learn as tiny babies: how to read the emotion on mother's face. This ability comes from the same root as empathy.

According to Kohut, 'the small child's perceptual merging with mother's face constitutes her most important access to mother's identity and her emotions' (1981, p.84). Our capacity for empathy originates in our earliest merger with mother whose feelings, actions and behaviours are included in the self. This primary empathy with mother prepares us for the recognition that the basic inner experiences of other people remain similar to our own. With psychopaths and some forms of personality disorder the capacity for empathy barely develops, with frightening results.

The empathic circuits within the brain

The intersubjective nature of the brain is facilitated by a system of neural mirroring in the brain. Mirror neurons discharge both when an action is performed and when a similar action is observed in another person. This seems to match the behaviour of others to our own experience. This enables us to reach some mutual understanding. So think for example of how you feel like yawning when someone near you yawns, or laughs, or feels sick. Have you ever been brought to tears simply by seeing someone else cry? When someone you love is feeling pain have you ever been almost able to feel that pain in your own body? As human beings we are designed to be able to feel our way into someone else's experiences; this gives us social and evolutionary advantage in that we can tell when someone is with us or against us – whether they are a potential danger or an ally.

The Streams in the Consulting Room

EMPATHY

Those of us who practise therapeutically tend to be well versed in empathising with others.

Pitfalls sometimes arise when the person we are trying to empathise with has behaved badly, what we see as immorally or in a way which damages others.

An old supervisor of mine in a prison setting first introduced me to the notion of separating the person from the behaviour. Even when faced with the worst of human behaviour, reminding ourselves that behind this lies real human suffering, woundedness and pain can help us to remain empathic even when full of revulsion, judgement or dislike.

Psychotherapy becomes a new attachment relationship (in adulthood) which is able to restructure attachment-related implicit memory through affective communication (non-verbal communication, undertones, atmosphere) more than verbal communication; thus the explicit past is not focused on as much but rather the implicit past which unconsciously organises and structures the client's 'procedural field' of relating to others. There is now a good deal of evidence (Badenoch 2008; Cozolino 2010; Gerhardt 2004) which suggests that the brain retains the capacity for re-organisation (or plasticity) well into adulthood and that new emotional experiences will help to restructure neural pathways in the pre-frontal cortex of the brain which controls social and emotional relationships. Significant parts of the emerging field of *interpersonal neurobiology* (Siegel 2012) consider how the relational world – both developmentally and therapeutically – shapes many of the neural structures that control emotional regulation, management of anxiety, stress and anger and our subjective experience of our psychosocial world.

I would urge you to read Professor Simon Baron-Cohen's fascinating book *Zero Degrees of Empathy* (2011) for more on the neuroscientific basis for empathy and what happens to those people who have little or none. He examines how a complete lack of empathy can present – among borderline, psychopathic and narcissistic patients – and how those with limited capacity for cognitive empathy but who are still able to feel affective empathy, such as those diagnosed with Asperger's Syndrome or those on the Autistic spectrum, are frequently misunderstood.

So empathy is the best tool we have for entering the internal psychological terrain of another person. It is one of the fundamental attributes that defines our humanity and is one of the key ingredients we have in our well. In many ways it is the oil that drives the engines of situatedness.

 The Key to EMPATHY is effort – to take that leap between your subjective experience of the world and imagining your way into theirs. Sometimes this comes naturally but effort is needed for the times it doesn't.

STREAM 16: TACIT KNOWLEDGE

We know more than we can tell.

Michael Polanyi (2009, p.4)

Tacit knowledge refers to skills and knowledge which lie deeply within our minds, our hands, our bodies, but of which we often struggle to give a verbal account. Like a painter who 'knows' which colours to mix to get the right effect or a mother who 'knows' exactly the tone of voice which will comfort her crying child. When we are in the apprentice stage we are constantly tested and interrogated on what we know, in exams, driving tests, the penetrating questions of the more experienced: this tends to make us feel anything coming from tacit knowledge is worthless unless it can be explained, justified or proven.

The more experienced you become, the less you need to make that tacit knowledge explicit, especially in the form of explaining yourself and what you are doing to someone else, who may be evaluating or questioning you. As this living water increases, as tacit knowing expands, this storehouse within us becomes far more than could ever be held at once in the conscious mind.

> ### Reflection Point
>
> **TACIT KNOWLEDGE**
>
> - *What does it feel like when you have to teach a complex activity which you 'know in your bones' to someone who is brand new to it?*
> - *What happens to your own skill level?*
> - *Think of half a dozen examples in your present life where you use excellent tacit knowledge which would look extraordinary to someone unskilled in the same field.*

Smith (2003) references the groundbreaking work of Michael Polanyi on tacit knowledge. Polanyi believed that acts of creativity – especially when they are undertaken in the spirit of discovery – are naturally imbued with powerful personal feelings and lead to a level of commitment on the part of the person involved. His best known text *Personal Knowledge* (1958) put forward a convincing critique of just how impersonal and (supposedly) value-free the scientific method was becoming (as practised in the West certainly). He sought to restore the value of 'tacit knowing' to the heart of the scientific endeavor. Smith highlights Polanyi's arguments that 'informed guesses, hunches and imaginings that are part exploratory acts are motivated by what he describes as "passions"'. His most famous quote is 'we know more than we can tell'. This approach captures beautifully the underlying ethos of situated action and practical wisdom and the real depth and richness it can bring to the practice of psychotherapy – not to replace models-led thinking, rather to humanise, enliven and ground it in the reality of face-to-face meeting which is experienced by us as emotional, physiological, temporal and spacial – as well as the purely cognitive. The scientific method has tended to reify the cognitive and mockingly exclude the other fields as somehow less than itself.

Restricting our view of the territory to a simple cognitive lens is likely to trip us up pretty fast in the lived experience of the human world. Sometimes this produces the phenomenon of stage fright: the actor who tacitly knows all five acts of *Hamlet* suddenly panics, and tries to remember it all to reassure himself he can do it. But as he fails to bring it all to mind, he freezes or, in similar vein, we leave the terrain and our situated action there for a time, and in that interval it all sinks down deep, we forget it consciously.

So we conclude we cannot do it, we've lost it, it has all leaked out of us...but in fact it is still there 'deep down'. Since it got there through active and conscious relating to the terrain, it is not until we are back in the terrain itself, and start to be alerted to all those sights, tastes, smells, sounds, again, and it is not until we start venturing into the action we once performed there, that the tacit knowing kicks in. Suddenly, 'it all floods back', we start to remember 'what we are doing', or 'how to do it', even though we don't know how we do it. And it is just as if we have never been away. This is why I have positioned the Leap of Faith as the first stream; until we have taken the leap the whole animal of situated – and tacit – knowing cannot bring itself to life.

Tacit knowledge is notoriously hard to pin down; mostly it cannot be written as sets of rules or procedures to be followed – you either have it or you don't – aesthetic sense, good taste, emotional intelligence, the ability to speak a language. Precisely because it cannot be made rule bound or abstract, models-led ways of thinking tend to be highly suspicious of it – indeed actively denigrate it in many cases. Despite this 'drawback' (from the models-led perspective) tacit knowledge goes on spectacularly doing what it does best: operating superbly in real-world terrain at the speed of light. Before a models-led mind can turn to the index page of the rulebook, tacit knowledge has finished and has its feet up enjoying a cup of tea.

We all experience forms of this tacit knowing daily: walking, brushing your teeth, playing sport, tying your shoelaces, driving, touch typing – through to the most complex forms of human activity: performing open heart surgery, conducting an orchestra, rock climbing, responding to a distressed child. Trying to stop and explain precisely how we were doing it would actively inhibit our ability – and that is why it is notoriously difficult to break down such skill into a set of idiot-proof rules.

> ### The Streams in the Consulting Room
>
> **TACIT KNOWLEDGE**
> Your store of tacit knowledge will build the longer you do work of this nature – it cannot be rushed or faked but must be nurtured, practised and eventually trusted.
>
> Likewise the client knows far more than they can tell – about what has hurt, or what keeps them stuck in old patterns or about how to heal and move forward – our job is to guide and support them in their discovery process and to help build the best space in which they can do this work for themselves.

Incidentally this is not simply true at the individual level. Tacit knowledge operates very strongly within groups and organisations. Hutchins (1996) gives a lovely example of this when he refers to the crew operating a large US aircraft carrier. Of the entire population on the bridge not one of them knows exactly everything that is going on. But as long as each of them performs the role they have been trained for, the ship operates smoothly. And here is the real point, to articulate and make explicit what we are doing at each stage of an operation would, in practice, slow us down and hamper us. The tacit knowledge is lying dormant inside our well, and when in the right domain it flows up out of us like a fountain.

 The Key to TACIT KNOWLEDGE is a decision to be open to your 'informed guesses, hunches and imaginings' as a profoundly valuable source of information when practising. Total reliance on trying to cognitively store the theoretical ideas of others will de-skill you in the end – even though it promises the opposite.

STREAM 17: HUMOUR

> Knowledge knows a tomato is a fruit; wisdom is not putting it in a fruit salad.
>
> Miles Kington

Just like Miles Kingston's gag above, humour carries with it profound truths, so has a place in the therapeutic world. It must, however, be used with finesse, as humour is a true double-edged sword. It can be one of the sweetest builders of a warm, connected therapeutic relationship, giving a shared language to both people in the dyad, giving moments of playful lightness and relief, taking the sting out of reliving painful memories and enabling both parties to share something creative, energised and real from their internal world.

On the other hand, used injudiciously, or poorly timed, a remark or laugh that feels too ambiguous can flatten the emotional energy of a session and leave it stone dead; it can sow seeds of mistrust and doubt or can reawaken traumatic memories of feeling shamed, humiliated, teased or mocked by others.

The Hungarian novelist Arthur Koestler in his 1964 classic *The Act of Creation* (Koestler 1989) argues that humour is the third element of creativity alongside discovery and art. The three sections of his book

– the Jester, the Sage and the Artist – explore the pivotal role discovery, imagination and humour have played in the great advances within both art and science; indeed he claims humans are at their most creative when rational thought is temporarily suspended, an idea that resonates perfectly with the situated operation of the practice wisdom streams.

Reflection Point

HUMOUR

- How did it feel when you had humour used against you as a weapon?
- Think of a time when something you meant humorously has been misinterpreted. What did the experience leave you with?
- How does the humour you use with your best friend differ from that used with your mother?
- In what sort of client situations would you feel extra cautious about employing humour?

Usually humour comes to us spontaneously as a natural reaction to something showing up in the intersubjective field. Given this, judging the appropriateness of a comment, tone of voice, chuckle or joke, can be tough to handle well as we think on our feet. How often does the true sting of a 'funny' comment only become apparent later – when someone is bruised, hurt or feels mocked because of it? Our intent in being humorous is often to bring us closer to others, to show our wit and cleverness, to find release and excitement in the company of others and simply to play. The darker side to humour is one we will rarely admit to: most of us don't like being caught with blood on our hands. When humour tips over into cruelty, mockery, snideness or sarcasm it can be experienced as wounding, excluding, judging – devastating – by those who feel like the target. If people have a long history of feeling like the butt of others' jokes they may be hypervigilant towards the underlying stab of humour's darker side, even perceiving innocent asides as containing hidden messages designed to wound them.

The less well we know people the greater the chance that what we feel is funny might injure them in ways we do not intend. This means that in therapy settings several key streams – slowing down, intuition and empathy – really need to be present when humour enters the therapy space. For me the riskier or edgier sort of laughs can only feel comfortable when we have a good, trusting bond already established. I also need to know the person's own humour style. If I pay close attention this usually becomes apparent early on, as does their relationship to humour in their childhood. Did they frequently experience humour used as a weapon against them? Do they have a deep history with embedded shame, feeling publicly humiliated, shy or highly anxious? Are there cultural, language or gender considerations which may increase the likelihood of misinterpretation of your intention by the client? Is the line of humour something you enjoy as a form of friendly banter with loved ones – and if so is it leaking into therapy space largely through habit?

The Streams in the Consulting Room

HUMOUR

Humour must be employed cautiously until we know the person fairly well – how sensitive, defensive or paranoid they are; and how robust their self-esteem. We need an idea of their basic moral framework and a sense of how they use language to express themselves.

It cannot be merely imposed by you or used to show off and build a kind of fake chumminess. If it evolves gradually, is shared and keenly alert to the client's responses it can be a wonderful way of relieving tension, conveying empathy and deepening your relationship.

If misjudged or mistimed, something that can serve as one of the best bonding elements of the relationship can turn into a minefield which can upset the building of trust and safety in both you and the therapy space.

We must also recognise the role that dark humour plays in dealing with life's tragedies. Years ago in my pre-psychology life I worked for the Crown Prosecution Service at London's famous Old Bailey court as a law clerk. In my first few days around the office not only was I presented with extremely gruesome photographs of murder victims and post-mortem processes each day on my return from lunch but was horrified to hear my colleagues joking and bantering about rape cases, murder victims and witnesses. At first I thought I might have wandered into an office staffed by callous psychopaths. When I finally reached the courtroom itself I overheard barristers, court officials, police officers and pathologists making the sickest of jokes which, if they had been heard by anyone involved in the case, victims or their relatives, would have been devastating and been rightly condemned as unbelievably insensitive. Gradually I found myself joining in with such dark humour with relish. Being regularly exposed to the utter depravity of which human beings are capable is overwhelming to the psyche and, if we are to continue functioning in such work, we need to find ways to cope and discharge. Later, working in the prison system, at an HIV/AIDS unit and with firefighters dealing with children who set fires, I have seen exactly the same humour emerge. It goes with the territory but is often misunderstood by those from outside. Henman (2008) examines the role humour played in the functioning of American servicemen who had been prisoners of war in Vietnam. She found it helped these men to feel as though they were fighting back and taking control over something unendurable. It helped to build resilience, especially as it served to build strong social support systems within the group, all of whom were encountering the same horrific and overwhelming phenomena.

Various forms of humour are used as defence mechanisms: laughing at myself before others can mock me, trying to show that my flaws and pain don't affect me too much, to convey strength in the face of adversity. Some clients have responded with self-deprecation, self-mockery or making light of their own pain, for so long that they are able to distance themselves effectively from feeling too much.

So early in therapy humour (used by me) will be warm, gentle and carefully non-controversial. I will watch and listen to see how my patient employs humour, and try to get a feel for the role humour has played in their life to date – and act accordingly, listening to my intuition and extending empathy to feel my way into their inner world as best I can. As the relationship deepens, trust builds and we simply know one another better – humour can morph into something unique and personal to this dyad. In using humour wisely we must take our time, feel our way slowly into its employment and be alert to the client's reactions and changes in the interpersonal field when either of us has used some 'funny'. If the client uses humour which seems unfeeling or intensely dark I try to understand its functions in their current psyche, even if I cannot find it funny myself.

So, dear reader, I think we know one another well enough by now – did you hear the one about a man walking in the street one day who was brutally beaten and robbed? As he lay unconscious and bleeding a therapist, who happened to be passing by, rushed up to him and exclaimed, 'My God! Whoever did this really needs my help!'

Or if that didn't do it for you: when the new patient was settled comfortably on the couch, the therapist began his therapy session. 'I'm not aware of your problem,' the therapist said. 'So perhaps you should start at the very beginning.'

'Of course,' replied the patient. 'In the beginning, I created the Heavens and the Earth...'

 The Key to HUMOUR is timing (just like comedy really) and to get it right you need to know your audience – so use carefully and sparingly near the start of the contract.

STREAM 18: WARMTH

All the statistics in the world can't measure the warmth of a smile.

Chris Hart (2009, p.28)

Chris Hart points out a truth that the rigidly models-led crowd really need to hear – maths and science cannot truly address human warmth. When you are feeling sad and in need of human comfort whom do you seek out? The man with a mountain of qualifications? Maybe the woman with the cleverest mind or perhaps those who understand theory with the best base of research evidence or the friend with the largest ego? For most of us what we need when we are feeling sad, alone, lost or disheartened is warm human connection. If we were lucky as babies we will have experienced warm, loving, attentive mothering (and fathering). When we were fed, held, rocked, smiled at and whispered to, our bodies and brains learned the comfort available from another human being, to down regulate, to relax. We learned to scan the face and the eyes for reassurance about how the other was really feeling about us, to tune into the emotional energy contained in their words, what we might call the voice of the heart or the music underneath the words. When that tone conveys judgement, criticism, coldness we feel it deeply – it pushes us away, shuts us down and can make us feel bad about ourselves.

Donald Winnicott (1971) called this process *mirroring* – looking into the face of another in order to really experience the self. He referred to the *gleam in the mother's eye* when she sees her child. This cannot be faked – humans are deeply skilled in assessing the truthfulness of the concerned face, the real feelings flowing within the tone of voice, the honesty of a smile. In the raw encounter of therapy, faking it almost guarantees failure.

Reflection Point

WARMTH

- *What emotional states do you associate with the word 'warmth'?*
- *Think of three memories that make you feel warm. What was so special about them?*
- *Now contrast with some memories where people left you feeling 'cold' – what emotions dominate here?*

Some unlucky children grow up with a world full of bad mirroring – a reflection which constantly tells them they are not good enough, problematic, too stupid, too ugly, a nuisance to have around. Even those of us who did not suffer so much were often deprived of enough *good mirroring* – to toughen us up, to ensure we did not become big-headed or vain, or simply because our parents didn't know how to do it very well.

The Streams in the Consulting Room

WARMTH

- Do not get too consumed with the myriad intricacies of therapeutic technique or theory.
- Do not hide behind the role of powerful expert in order to handle your own fears and nervousness.
- Do not fall for the lie that cold aloofness equates to true professionalism.
- Much of the residual pain we carry with us from childhood stems from times when the right kind of warmth was not available to us – that will never be truly healed in the absence of genuine warmth from you during therapy.

Many people who come to us as therapists will have been wounded by a lack of human warmth in their lives, or warmth only on offer under certain conditions or that came with a high price attached. They may have struggled to develop the quality of warmth within themselves, showing the world only brittle, chilly armour. The very last thing this person needs when they come to work with me is someone projecting cold, aloof expertise, hiding behind rigid technique or the perfect *blank screen*. In my opinion much damage was done by orthodox psychoanalytic practitioners in the 1940s and 1950s (immediately after the death of Freud) whose only concern was to encourage the projection of transferential material onto the blank screen. They really believed the screen was a neutral space which was a useful tool in eliciting the central curative factor in analysis – transference.

In order to gradually melt ice there is no point putting the ice cube into the freezer. People have to feel safe in therapeutic space – after all they are likely to be expressing emotions connected to fear, anger, shame or loss – feeling unloved or never good enough. Most of us already have a loud enough critical voice in our heads, we don't need it reinforced externally.

Being a warm therapist does not mean being overly soppy or sentimental, however; at times our clients will need honesty from us, challenge, containment and boundary. All of these can still be delivered with warmth and concern. Heinz Kohut (1981) called this 'optimal frustration' and argued that this represents the ideal conditions for personal growth: enough support to help us not feel alone or invisible, together with a bracing honesty that requires us to take responsibility for doing more of the work of life ourselves as we grow older and more independent.

Most people walking into a first session are not coming because the world feels too warm towards them or because they are able to speak to themselves in a warm, soothing, respectful way. The adult world in which we exist is all too full of coldness, harshness, duplicity, concealment and lack of genuine concern for our well-being. As I frequently say to my students – people don't come to therapy because they are too happy.

Many childhoods were the same. The therapist – and the potential space she co-creates with the client – must never replicate this. It should feel interested, attentive, holding, human and warm. In this safe space the exploration of the darker parts of self can unfold. In a freezer most of us will close down, protect ourselves and withdraw; in gentle sunshine we tend to relax, soften and open up; in glaring heat we burn, sweat and redden.

Like Goldilocks' porridge, the therapist cannot be too hot or too cold – we must try to get it just right. Sylvia Plath, in her *Unabridged Journals* put it beautifully:

> How we need that security. How we need another soul to cling to; another body to keep us warm. To rest and trust; to give your soul in confidence: I need this. I need someone to pour myself into. (2002, p.102)

 The Key to WARMTH is meaning it. Human beings are pretty good at detecting fake warmth – so don't even try. The real thing is the only one that matters.

CHAPTER 4
SPECIAL EQUIPMENT

- Juggling
- Improvisation
- Digging
- Intersubjectivity
- Presence
- Bravery
- Creativity

There are times on the road towards practical wisdom where we meet obstacles, blockages, find direction signs that lead us the wrong way, get lost, become discouraged or simply trip ourselves up by trying to do too much at once. As we are dealing with the unfamiliar and the unexpected the only thing we can confidently expect is that it will all go wrong occasionally and we have to work hard to find a way through. A later section explores some of these in more depth – what I have called the

'Rip Tides' – that may unbalance us when diving deeper. At these times we may need to draw upon some special kit to help us get through. This set of streams will not necessarily be part of the toolkit of the beginner but the more confident we can become in using them the wiser our practice will be.

STREAM 19: JUGGLING

The world cannot be governed without juggling.

John Selden

In essence this stream is about being able to multi-task, to keep many balls in the air at once, without dropping them. The pressured, busy lives we often lead today require this skill from us in many situations. It is the fear of dropping the ball that gives a sense of strain and stress to so many of our endeavours. As experienced situated practitioners we need to be able to function effectively whilst juggling many streams of information, both emotional and practical, whilst in session with clients and also whilst developing ourselves into master craftspeople.

One of the most daunting aspects of a therapy session, especially when you are still training or on a day when your energy and attention levels are not at their best, is trying to stay present and attuned to the multiple streams of information, feeling and activity which are flowing through the field. First, there is the flow inside of you: your countertransference responses, your empathic reaction to the client's material (and weighing up whether this feeling is in fact empathic or countertransferential), how your body is feeling that day, things that may be happening in your own life which are pulling your emotional focus, thoughts about theories, incidents with other clients which may remind you of something happening in the here and now, a memory of a hunch about this client that you noted last session, that deep feeling of being profoundly moved by the content of their story.

In addition there will be a flood of material coming from the interpersonal field, the intersubjective realm operating in the space between you. You may be 'keeping an eye on' your understanding of how this client's personality is structured, how the story they are currently telling you may illuminate aspects of this, thinking about how you might reflect some of this back to them, how to gently phrase an interpretation so that they are able to make best use of it. You may be considering some aspect of theory which might shape your next response, or listening closely to the tone of voice or facial expression employed when the client is sharing with you. Watching how their body moves and tuning into the sadness, wistfulness, joy or anxiety being expressed in the room. And this is even before we begin to pay attention to the actual words flowing back and forth between us, our eye contact, our smiles and laughter.

The process of attempting to tune in as accurately as we can to what is going on in the client's internal emotional world, what it feels like to be them experiencing this memory, this feeling, this lived reality – the very act of empathy – is not easy at first. We need to place our focus on trying to catch all this as best we can. I would liken it to trying to gradually tune in a radio dial to the right frequency, a subtle and ongoing process that demands therapist sensitivity, attention and concentration. It is partly this factor which makes a whole run of back-to-back therapy sessions so draining.

> ### The Streams in the Consulting Rooom
>
> **JUGGLING**
>
> I sometimes use the metaphor of the fighter pilot when describing to students how a therapy session can feel – we must pay attention to multiple streams of visual, auditory, kinaesthetic and intellectual information at the same time, sensing which to privilege, trying to analyse their meaning, noting transferential material, thinking about whether that feeling we are having is empathic, countertransferential or something of both – all the while trying to 'stay' with the client.
>
> There are lots of spinning plates and only one of us. The skills of learning to juggle all this take time to settle into our bones – the training practitioner (or the recently qualified) can feel heavily overwhelmed (as, at times, can those of us who have been doing it for many years!).
>
> The only real 'cure' for this is practice – learning to trust your reflexive and responsive self in the complexity of such territory is not achieved overnight so give yourself permission to drop the ball now and then without punishing yourself.

So how is it possible for us to attend to so many things at one time and make a reasonable – although never perfect – job of it? From the outside, much like watching someone juggle five balls or five clubs, it seems incredible. And even from outside the session, to the therapist herself, it may seem extraordinary that she is able to do this over and over again – the fear kicks in when we try to explain something in rational, intellectual terms which is coming from a mysterious, unconsciously intelligent place.

The Therapeutic Loom

The really extraordinary thing about these threads of activity, feeling and information is how they weave together so well in the midst of situated flow. And, when it is working well, we don't have to actively think about how we are doing it. Rather it becomes something holistic, the sum much greater than its individual parts. This is like watching an experienced weaver pull together disparate threads of colour and texture into amazing patterns at such speed that we can no longer see what is happening at the micro level. We see similar fluid, rapid pattern making in schools of fish, flocks of birds or herds of animals. This is skill in action, an embodied intelligence which is expressing itself physically, energetically, verbally, in real space and time. And now we need to ask ourselves the biggest question about juggling and situatedness: *do we even need to know how it works?*

Now a certain mindset (models-led naturally) will not be satisfied that something really works until they have dismantled, deconstructed, poked, prodded, examined, listed and categorised it. Trusting in something happening in such an unexplained, natural, dare we say, magical, way is not to their taste. It unnerves them. They are reluctant to leave phenomena sitting under the soft, complementary glow of candlelight when they could be subjected to the harsh, interrogatory glare of full electric light. From a research perspective this may make some sense – but in practice this desperate need for total and complete transparency may be counterproductive.

Reflection Point

JUGGLING

- *Where do you have to do the most juggling in your life at present?*
- *What helps you come to decisions about which items to put down? (If you ever manage to do that!)*
- *What do you notice when you observe other people trying to juggle too much?*
- *Do you feel we can model how to manage complexity for our clients? If so, think of some examples.*

In the heat of the moment it can hamper you to think about the fact that you are actually doing what you are doing. This is much like a small child learning to ride the bike: they will have a brief moment where their mum or dad lets go of the back of the bike and they are riding themselves, then they realise it's actually happening and they instantly doubt their ability to do the very thing they have just been doing. Then the bike wobbles and they fall off. Trying to stand back and observe what we are doing, or categorise or analyse it, in the midst of creative or situated flow tends to knock us off balance. Anyone who presents, acts or teaches – in fact any performance in front of an audience – will tell you that one of the most unnerving things that can happen to you is that split second when you cross over into a type of out-of-body experience. Where you are almost watching yourself perform this complex activity and have that terrifying jolt where you have to push yourself back 'in body' again. The over-monitoring of self and the activity, while it is happening, becomes a serious obstacle. If a soldier rushing into battle, or a fire-fighter racing into a burning building when everyone else is running in the opposite direction, stopped to really think about what they were doing it is highly likely they would not be able to carry on.

A juggler could tell you this. If you break your concentration to think about how you are juggling the balls, they are on their way to the floor – fast. The skilled juggler learns to intuitively work with the balls and the air and their hands and eyes; thinking is counterproductive. Jung was astute when putting it like this: 'Often the hands will solve a mystery that the intellect has struggled with in vain' (1985, p.181). There are many times deep inside terrain when it is the body that must act in the split second, to bring the mind into play merely serves to hinder our right action. We also know, however, that out body can feel like our worst enemy at times of uncertainty or stress: it floods with adrenaline as our amygdala triggers the fight-or-flight mechanism. As part of our journey towards true situated action we must learn how to incorporate the body as a central part of what we are doing.

 The Key to JUGGLING is honesty with yourself about your level of juggling skill – trying to manage more than you are able because you feel you should is only likely to lead to disaster.

STREAM 20: IMPROVISATION

> These are days when no one should rely unduly on his competence. Strength lies in improvisation. All the decisive blows are struck left-handed.
>
> Walter Benjamin

When the well is operating most powerfully there is a productive flow of thought and feeling that is playing, creating and shaping in the moment. It comes from a place that is, in fact, beyond thinking, beyond planning and outside of conscious choosing. It shows up just at the right moment, just in reach and works perfectly to move things on, unpack new truths or to throw fresh light on something previously shrouded and dark.

We are talking about the capacity for improvisation. It is inevitably somewhat frightening. In the midst of a therapy session or a performance on stage or on the sports pitch there emerges a blank space, an empty moment, a gap which I do not quite know how to fill. This can make us tense up as we feel the responsibility for finding something appropriate to put in place. Over time and as experience starts to really fill your well you will begin to trust that when the bucket dips down into the water something good will come back up. The anxiety stems from the fact that the bucket could rise up empty or containing the wrong thing. And this is the risk that we must learn to embrace: when we improvise we can sometimes fail or fall, embarrass ourselves in front of others, get it all wrong. However, sometimes what appears will be new, exciting, different, profoundly generative or creative.

Reflection Point

IMPROVISATION

- *What happens to your body, your thoughts and your emotions when you have to think on your feet?*
- *Are there areas of your life where you enjoy the creativity of improvising and other areas where you dread it? What is the difference between the two?*
- *Think of someone whose improvisational skill you admire – what do you see them doing that you could work on for yourself?*

One of the great ironies that situated practice points towards is that models which promise us predictability and safety whilst in new terrain actually handicap us and make us more likely to crash and burn. Sometimes literally so: in 1995 a commuter jet flying from Atlanta airport in the US lost power in one engine shortly after take-off. The pilot assumed the engine had failed. Both he and his co-pilot kept a watchful eye on their instrument panel, as the emergency manual told them to do, which was telling them the engine had simply stalled. In actual fact the engine had exploded and was pulling the plane dangerously off course as its climb towards cruising altitude failed. Eventually something in the pilot's intuition told him that the instruments were not telling the whole story. He turned his head and looked out of the window. What he saw, the tattered remnants of an exploded engine, was terrifying but very instructive. It enabled him to ignore the flow of false information the plane's technology was feeding him and to start to improvise in the moment, using all of his experience, senses and knowledge to bring the plane to a crash landing. Sadly, some of his passengers died, but many survived and would not have done so had he not been able to abandon the model before him and improvise.

And this point is vital for us in our understanding of situatedness. We need to be able to change our behaviour in the midst of changing circumstances, to respond creatively in the moment. The field in which we operate is rarely static; it may be predictable eight times out of ten but if we are not open to a total switch on that ninth or tenth time we will be thrown by it. Also we must realise that our actions will have unforeseen consequences on the field itself. As much as we are affected by the field, the field can also be affected by us. This is the truth of intersubjectivity and co-creation. Nothing in our experience forms in a vacuum. It grows from our contact with the field, in the space between us.

Improvisation for the new kid on the block

There is a harsh truth about improvisation. The more experienced you are the easier it is. The flip side of this, naturally, is that when you are brand new to something it is harder to do. Our brave pilot, had he been taking his first ever flight, is unlikely to have responded so well. Whilst it would be foolish to ignore this truth there is a much more positive side to it. When you are brand new to something, others around you rarely expect you to be perfect straight away. It is in tasting and trying, sampling and playing that we begin to discover what feels right for us and where our strengths and interest lie. In the meantime we know that central to the situated mindset is the lack of expectation of outcome – at some profound level we are meant to be lost at first. The real master craftsman in any field will often take improvisation to a whole new level. They will dare to walk on the narrowest part of the high ridge. Part of the fascination with watching someone who is a true genius at their art is that they could fall off the high wire at any moment. Our excitement is generated by knowing that they may either soar to new heights or drop to the floor. This is why our heart stays in our mouth as we watch them and why they generate such passion in their audience. We get to vicariously taste the danger and the risk and we love them for being willing to go there on our behalf. Most fields of human endeavour are packed full of competent, reliable, functional and efficient practitioners who rarely screw up but who rarely reach the great heights either. Meanwhile the stars, those who break new ground and push the boundaries, aren't reliable and dependable: in fact they embody the exact opposite: think George Best, Marlon Brando, Billie Holliday, Wayne Rooney, Mario Balotelli, Vincent Van Gogh, Robin Williams, Amy Winehouse, Kurt Cobain, Ella Fitzgerald, John Lennon, Norman Mailer, Rudolf Nureyev, Maria Callas – many of the exceptional people in artistic fields are exciting precisely because they could go over the edge at any minute (as some of them did).

Now I am not encouraging you to live life in quite such a daredevil way. Therapy is not rock and roll and should not be practised recklessly. But to have the courage to sometimes walk closer to the edge than we thought possible can be wonderfully creative, stretching us and opening us up to new skills, capacities and talents. We must be able to bear the risk and embrace adventure.

The Streams in the Consulting Room

IMPROVISATION

The experienced practitioner already knows that they have to improvise constantly. The student believes that when they are fully qualified they will know exactly what to do at each and every moment.

In our work at the university we encourage our under-graduates to play with the idea of improvising in many areas of life. If we try to script something too much in advance – an interview, a tricky phone call to someone after a fight, how to deal with a new-born baby – it never works.

We feel we cannot think on our feet when it matters because anticipatory anxiety gets the better of us – we must learn to be aware of such anxiety but press on anyway and not believe its negative and confidence-destroying whispers and lies.

The Key to IMPROVISATION is learning your craft so well that it lives in your heart, your bones and your gut – once the journey down the main road is mastered you can begin to branch off down side alleyways and release your natural creativity.

STREAM 21: DIGGING

It is no use asking me or anyone else how to dig... Better to go and watch a man digging, and then take a spade and try to do it.

Gertrude Jekyll

After many years of practice, I still find it somewhat extraordinary that someone can walk into my consulting room, meet a complete stranger and within minutes be talking about some of the most intimate, painful and distressing aspects of their lives. Of course not everybody treats these first few moments the same. Some clients will burst into tears the minute they sit down in the chair, the months of tense emotional build-up to this moment overwhelming them. Others will be very polite, cheerful and light-hearted, whilst others will report the difficult and distressing things happening to them but without very much emotion in their voice, and with very little eye contact, almost as though they were telling a story about someone else.

In training as counsellors and psychotherapists we are often taught to look for the client's presenting problem. This is the reason why clients say they are coming to some form of therapeutic help. Outside of the Western world it is commonly understood that when people are struggling with psychological or emotional difficulties they will often come to doctors or a Shaman or community healers and refer to the physical manifestations of what they're feeling. In other words, a headache may be reported or a stomach problem or the fact that they feel tired all the time. These things become metaphors for deeper underlying problems which are perhaps more difficult to talk about and which may be heavily socially stigmatised. In Western psychological thinking we recognise these matters as being of a psychosomatic origin. Freud, with his mainly female patients suffering from 'hysteria' and conversion disorders, was very aware of this particular problem. In setting out this stream – Digging – I am suggesting that the presenting problem is rarely the real thing or the only thing troubling this person. For sure, some clients will come to therapy and begin by originally talking about their tiredness or how their anxiety manifests in the form of palpitations or headaches. However, this is a much broader issue than merely converting psychological problems into the reporting of physical ones.

The Streams in the Consulting Room

DIGGING
We need to stay aware that what clients report – especially near to the start of the work – may represent a mere scratching at the surface of what really ails them. They may be ashamed, terrified, embarrassed, cautious or anxious about revealing how they feel behind the myriad of social masks and defences we all employ.

The root of psychological suffering may lie in their unconscious mind, their deepest memory stores, or be split, regressed, projected or denied.

Frequently people will use visual metaphors of locked boxes, cellars or closed-off rooms where the most painful or troubling of material remains.

Like an archaeologist we must dig slowly, carefully and patiently to reach the underground places where real healing can occur.

When we first walk into therapy space we will often feel tremendously vulnerable, afraid, lost or embarrassed. The over-riding feeling of needing to ask a professional for help may be one of guilt, shame or deep-seated fear, depending on what we have been socialised to believe. When we are teaching under-graduate psychology and counselling students we try to build in many experiential exercises to the modules. This is to give the students a deeper, more visceral, sense of what that vulnerability actually feels like. The moment we choose to drop some of our masks and defences and reveal some of our inner vulnerable self to another human being is a truly profound one. To do that in the context of a relationship with a professional person that one has never met before only increases the psychological burden at hand. Therapists should never forget this. This is one reason why I believe that any training for counsellors, psychotherapists, counselling psychologists or clinical psychologists should include a period of time when the trainee is receiving some form of psychotherapeutic help for themselves. If nothing else, it gives them an appreciation of what it feels like to sit in that other chair, which they will never forget.

For all of these reasons, it's important for the therapist to realise that the initial moments of revelation, indeed, the first few sessions, are very likely to be only scraping the surface in terms of psychological wounds, struggles, personal blind spots and difficult memories. I have lost count of the number of times that during the initial session the client has reported a very uneventful and broadly happy childhood. Indeed, this is so common, that in my supervision group we almost always raise an eyebrow when somebody reports that the client has said this to them during an assessment. Very often the parts of childhood that really wounded, rejected or upset the person are either blocked off or repressed or, more commonly, they are wary about revealing the real magnitude of these feelings up front. They may fear being judged, or it may simply be the case that it's difficult to verbalise these feelings, because they represent something which the person has tried to avoid for so long.

Usually in a medium- to long-term piece of work, I expect some of the deeper fault lines of the personality to begin revealing themselves only gradually, once a trusting, safe, relational space has been built between us. So the disclosure of secrets, the deepening of early themes, and sometimes complete changes of direction are to be expected along the way. The canny therapist knows this and keeps the picture of this person's story fairly open in their mind because new colours, shades and images are almost bound to reveal themselves as the journey progresses. Interestingly the subconscious mind seems to have a series of very handy images and metaphors to describe this material which is 'walled off' or 'repressed' as the Freudians would have it. It has shown up in my therapy work as a cellar, a locked box, a cupboard they are too scared to open, an underground toxic river which they feel is slowly poisoning them, and a dam of ice behind which is stored a dark, powerful wall of water which they fear will overwhelm and drown them. When we describe 'resistance' to the therapeutic task this is often what we are really witnessing, a desperate psychological attempt to keep at bay those things which harmed, terrified, hurt or angered the client during childhood. A complex system of psychological defences or 'survival strategies' may have been built to keep these toxic and frightening memories, feelings and thoughts outside of their conscious awareness. Of course it may be that very defence system, built at a time when the child felt herself to be trying to survive within a battlefield with little option for escape, fighting back or exercising any real power or control over the situation, that is now harming or constricting the adult person to an unbearable degree. It should be noted that convincing the inner child to let go of that defensive armour is easier said than done. However, that is one of the major tasks facing the therapy dyad if long-term characterlogical change is going to occur.

Reflection Point

DIGGING

- *Try to visualise the part of your mind where the darker material lies – what Jung called 'the shadow'.*
- *If it were a physical place what would it look like?*
- *How do you see it? How does it feel when you think about it?*
- *Are there some parts of it that would be too overwhelming to ever share with another person? Some that are even too much to acknowledge to yourself?*

One of the classic complaints I hear very frequently in therapy is adults saying that they don't understand why they continue to behave in certain ways. Usually, if we are choosing Option A on a frequent basis and yet Option A is continuing to hurt us or make life difficult, in my experience that is usually because there's an Option B lurking somewhere in our unconscious mind, which we feel will be even worse. For example, why does a woman remain in an abusive relationship, year after year, when many of the people around her may well be pleading with her to leave this man and go on to a new life? Why does the smoker continue smoking, year after year, when they're told repeatedly by friends, health professionals and media messages that what they are doing is killing them? Why does the heroin addict continue to inject? Why does a workaholic continue to sell themselves body and soul to their job even when they knows it is damaging their health, family and relationships? Why does the obsessive-compulsive continue to check and wash and monitor and hoard, even though it is driving them to the point of insanity? There is only one reason of course. That is because they fear that if they stop this behaviour something even worse lies ahead. They believe that if they open their locked box (or cellar door) what lies beneath their conscious mind may destroy them. As Hilaire Belloc's Jim discovered when a lion ate him after running away from his guardian at the zoo – 'And always keep a-hold of Nurse / For fear of finding something worse' (2009 [1907]).

This speaks to our 'anticipatory anxiety' – which features in the background of so much human behaviour, especially the anxiety disorders and relationship decisions. Let's take the case of the abused woman, who stays in a very difficult and violent relationship. Usually, when we strip things away, we can see underneath a terror of loneliness or a fear that they may not know how to survive on their own, or indeed dread that the partner may come after them and make things even worse. So in other words, this person is carrying a belief that: 'I have to put up with what I have now, because it's not as bad as what may lie ahead of me or because I feel I could not continue in the event of losing something I now have'. In models of psychotherapeutic work such as CBT, these are referred to as 'limiting beliefs', under which we usually find a very deep-seated layer of driving fears. The ultimate fear may be that people won't like them, it may be that they will be abandoned and left alone, or that they won't get to feel special and wonderful any more when they have to realise how simply ordinary they are. For the schizoid client, it may be that they have to open up to the terrors of intimacy and actually feeling something. For the addict it may well be that these years of maladaptive self-soothing behaviours, which show up in their addiction, are something for them to focus on rather than facing the terrifying emptiness, loneliness or thoughts of losing control which may be running underneath.

The longer these patterns have been in place, the more habitual behaviours will become. It is usually harder to shift these patterns of behaviour, thinking and feeling when people are in their fifties not their twenties. The situated therapist learns early on that to make genuine progress clients have to dig below the surface of their thoughts, feelings and behaviours. Like a garden it is easy to become fascinated by the beauty of the flowers above ground, but if we do not attend to the health and shape of the root system below ground the garden will not remain healthy for long. So the wise therapist needs to dig – cautiously, carefully and sensitively for sure – but dig we must if we are to uncover the real psychological drivers of human behaviour.

 The Key to DIGGING is patience and sensitivity balanced with a desire to see if another layer lies beneath what is being presented – and to understand why that layer may presently need to be defended by the psyche.

STREAM 22: INTERSUBJECTIVITY

What intersubjectivity means for the situated practitioner

In life there is not just you. Your sense of self is constantly in interaction, sometimes in dialogue, with everything else that is outside of you. This includes other people and the whole physical, spiritual and energetic world: you and the rest of the universe. You are affected by it and it is affected by you. Even though our existential aloneness is a fact of life with which we must all come to terms, we experience this aloneness in a sea of others. This can sometimes make it even harder to bear.

The radical subjectivist sees this dilemma in the following way: the truth is we are imprisoned within our separate bodies like small boats bobbing silently on a vast ocean. We can only experience the world from the perspective of our own boat. We may well be aware of the other boats nearby on the water and the occupants of those boats can try to tell us what it is like in their craft, but we can never really know. The only truth is the one we can experience. Taken to its farthest extreme, this position is the one taken up by the psychopath. Only my experience is real and others are only objects there to affect, sustain or be subsidiary to me. This position lacks all empathy for the real experience of others.

The radical objectivist position believes that we can look at the other boats, measure them, categorise them, study them and by applying certain scientific rules to this endeavour come to know the truth about being inside the other boats. The danger of this position in its extreme form is that we begin making ever bigger assumptions and arrogantly feel that we know the truth of others' realities just by engaging in scientific, religious or political categorisation. This stance often devalues emotional experience precisely because it cannot be tested and measured in a scientifically valid way. It begins to insist there is only one truth, one book, one God, one chosen people, one race, one view, one life that really matters. Taken to its limit it eventually justifies the repression, the expulsion, the incarceration, the murder of anyone who does not fit that one view. This position also lacks all empathy for the real experience of others.

The intersubjective position is different. It acknowledges that I have a subjective truth but it accepts that you have a subjective truth too. And in the space where we meet something occurs that has the potential to change both of us. It is in this space that communication, dialogue, empathy and connection are born. This is the ground from which love and friendship springs, and music, art, sex, debate, teaching, philosophy, storytelling. In fact most of what is best about us as human beings. It is also, of course, where the therapeutic encounter happens. It is mysterious and new. It is a place which neither of us could reach on our own. We can only be in this place together. And in the connection that happens between us while we are in this space both of us may have experiences, feelings, gain knowledge or make discoveries that we take away with us when we leave and return to the world of self.

During infancy we are barely able to understand that there is anything outside of this place of connectedness, it feels more like a merger or symbiosis between us and our primary caregiver. D. W. Winnicott (1971) developed an idea of a primordial 'intermediate space' between mother and baby, inner psyche and outer world, where inner and outer are combined and mixed up. For him this was a play space, an imaginary yet real space, fluid enough to be open to dialogue and negotiation with other people.

SPECIAL EQUIPMENT

> ### Reflection Point
>
> **INTERSUBJECTIVITY**
>
> - Think of someone in your life who is very different from you but with whom it feels comfortable to acknowledge and share your polarised subjectivity of the world.
> - Now think of someone where you always seem to misunderstand one another, rub each other up the wrong way, no matter how hard you try to get them to see your point of view.
> - Why do you feel there is a difference? What changes inside you when you are with these two different people? How do your thoughts, feelings and behaviour change?

Dialogue, intersubjectivity and the growth of the emotional brain

Furthermore there is good neuroscience to now back this up. As we touched on briefly in the Intuition stream earlier we are living through a period where we are deepening our understanding that the capacity for relationship, empathy, self-regulation (and much else) gets hard-wired into the brain on the basis of early relational experience. In the last 15 years neuroscience has been taking giant leaps forward in helping us to understand how we 'catch' another person's emotional state. In 1996 Italian neuroscientists (Gallese, Fadiga, Fogassi and Rizzolatti) were studying grasping behaviour in monkeys. Electrodes were attached to the monkey's brain to determine which neurons fired when it grasped things. One day a hungry researcher reached out for some raisins. Simultaneously neurons in the monkey's brain fired. They noticed these were the exact same neurons which fired when the monkey grasped the raisins itself. They discovered connector cells, since named 'mirror neurons'. This lends a whole new dimension to our understanding of empathy, countertransference and projective identification. It shows how we can deeply feel our way into another person's experience. In that sense emotion really can be infectious. When somebody else's mood brings you up or brings you down it may be that the mirror neurons in your brain are firing on all cylinders.

> ### The Streams in the Consulting Room
>
> **INTERSUBJECTIVITY**
> We must understand the realities of intersubjectivity if we are ever to develop into an empathic therapist.
>   The ability to temporarily put aside, interrogate or observe our own window on the world is vital if we are to stand any chance of seeing life through the window of the suffering person sitting in front of us.
>   We have to slip our own skin for a while and try to see things from another's term of reference, imagining ourselves into human experiences which may seem alien, frightening or strange – or which we may have been taught to condemn.
>   The wise practitioner is able to make these journeys into the being of another – never perfectly or precisely to be sure – but with the right intention and a willingness to situate away from the self it becomes surprisingly easy.

The development of capacity for empathy has its origins in a child's original caregiving relationships (Gerhardt 2004). Allan Schore demonstrates the effect of emotional experience on the pre-frontal cortex of a baby's developing brain. Positive emotional experience with the parent triggers pleasurable endorphins and dopamine which affect the pre-frontal cortex. So the looks and smiles of a loving parent actually help the brain to grow in a social, emotionally intelligent way. Cozolino (2010) gives the example of adults who were once the children of anxious parents. He says that when such a child is small they will return again and again to their parents for a sense of safety and security. They will be repeatedly disappointed. The parent will be unable to act as a soothing, containing object for the child as they are too concerned with managing their own anxiety. The child will not be helped in learning to self-soothe and their brain will be deficient in its self-regulatory capacity. Cozolino points out that that many of these children in effect become parents to their own parents: the source of soothing for others rather than the recipients of it.

Interestingly he also uses the metaphor of the well: 'the repeated return to an empty well. Each time the bucket is lowered there is the hope that it will contain the nurturance they need when it is raised. Each time the bucket comes up empty it reinforces the basic lack of dependability of relationships and safety in the world'.

Such prematurely grown children miss out on a vital stage of childhood. They show up in therapy in large numbers: often stuck in a pattern of chronic over-caretaking of others whilst feeling abandoned and hungry themselves. It should be plain to see that some in this group of youngsters are likely to grow up to be effective therapists, very able to see into the emotional world of others and assist in soothing it. It is from this template that the 'wounded healer' is formed.

 The Key to INTERSUBJECTIVITY is humility. I am not always right, frequently I am wrong. I might not have experienced the same as someone else and therefore my beliefs, values, reactions and sympathies are very likely to be different from theirs. If I learn to observe and question myself I am part way to situating myself in the shoes of another.

STREAM 23: PRESENCE

Few delights can equal the *presence* of one woman we trust utterly.

George MacDonal

Probably one of the oldest debates within psychotherapy revolves around the role of the psychotherapist. Back in the 1940s, the hard-line Freudian psychoanalysts tried incredibly hard to be the blank screen, neutral analyst. No self-disclosure was allowed and countertransference was seen as positively destructive. Indeed, it was preferable that the analyst say very little at all, just occasionally offering an interpretation to the patient. The humanistic movement of the 1960s onwards, through the development of therapeutic models such as Carl Rogers' person-centred theory (2004 [1961]), encouraged a rebalancing of power between the client and the therapist and saw genuineness, congruence and unconditional positive regard as being the *sine qua non* of good psychotherapy. The role of detached medical expert was to be dropped in favour of genuine equality with the client and personal self-disclosure was encouraged to show the client that you too were a suffering human being, just the same as them.

> ### Reflection Point
>
> **PRESENCE**
>
> - How can you tell when someone is only pretending to be fully present with you? What do you notice? How do you feel?
> - Think of the people in your family of origin – from which one did you feel the most genuine presence? What effect did that have on you psychologically as you grew?
> - And what of those who felt emotionally or psychologically absent even when physically present? How do you remember them and the way they have shaped your life?

These days in the UK, with the rise to dominance of CBT within the National Health Service, the central importance of warm therapeutic relationship is being somewhat diminished in favour of short-term, evidence-based collaboration between the suffering individual and their graduate mental health worker. I have always passionately believed that the two extremes of the therapeutic role are both damaging in their different ways. The clinical, authoritarian stance of the classical psychoanalytic therapist could often prove very traumatic for anyone whose childhood had been experienced at the hands of a cold, abusive or distant parent. Even those of us lucky enough to have much warmer parental relationships often found the traditional blank slate therapist as being anything other than therapeutic.

Meanwhile at the wilder, hippier edges of the person-centred movement we can find therapists afraid to challenge, overly worried about setting an agenda and desperate to not offend or upset at any cost. Over the years I have heard this described as nodding dog therapy, all reflecting back and concerned looks, but very little else. Many clients who have come to me, after prolonged exposure to this type of work, found it hugely frustrating and felt they were getting very little from it. One rather unkindly, yet perhaps noticing a kernel of truth, described it as like being with a very kind vicar on Valium. Naturally this only characterises the very worst practitioners within this type of model. And, let's face it: all models have their appallingly bad practitioners.

> ### The Streams in the Consulting Room
>
> **PRESENCE**
>
> It is never OK to be psychologically absent during therapy sessions – I feel presence is one of the most important streams because human beings are so alert to it being faked or given grudgingly.
>
> We may feel we are getting away with it when our mind wanders to the shopping list, or to the fun we had last weekend, or too deeply into our own sadness, fear or loss but the client will sense it and is likely to interpret your leaving of them in a negative way which may very well reinforce the lack of loving, empathic presence they struggled with in past relationships.
>
> In truth, if they are paying us or not, we have made a promise to be fully present to try to be empathically attuned and to provide a safe, containing space in which they can try to heal. An intermittently present therapist is breaking that promise.
>
> When our mind occasionally strays – as it will – we must strive to bring ourselves back to our client. Practice helps here – as it does with everything else!

This is one of those streams that should be absolutely essential for any therapist. In fact, I get rather angry when I hear of therapists who do not use it well. So what do I mean by really showing up? Surely if I'm sitting in the room, physically present and nodding and head tilting in all the right places, that means I am there, doesn't it? I sometimes wonder if therapists who are happy to see 20, 25 or 30 clients a week really believe this to be true. Really showing up for the client means working very hard to stay present, focused and emotionally attuned throughout the whole session. It means working hard to put aside one's own current worries, tiredness and the thousand mental distractions, to which we can all fall prey. It means juggling many balls of information, knowledge and emotion, to keep working hard to make links between what's happening in the room right now, what's going on in the client's current life and linking back to the original relational patterns of their childhood. It means hard work.

The best therapists manage to find a space for working with clients, where they can be real, concerned, warm and very present, without ever abandoning the role of repairing and somewhat more knowledgeable parent, which I personally believe lies at the heart of the therapeutic endeavour. The young child does not want their parents to simply be another child, alongside them. At the same time, they do not want their parent to be distant, cold and seemingly unconcerned. They need a warm and loving active presence, which is not afraid to set boundaries, impose discipline where necessary and pass on, to the best of their ability, any particular knowledge or experience, which is relevant to the child's situation at the time: authoritative, rather than authoritarian or permissive parenting.

The needs of the psychotherapy client, and the aim of the good therapist, are fundamentally no different. Daniel Siegel (2012) defines presence as 'an emergent property of our existence in which we are open and receptive to ourselves and to others, ready to receive and ready to connect' (p.173). The two-way nature of presence is clear from this: we need to be attuned to and aware of the self as well as the other and, like a two-way radio, able to receive information as well as transmit.

I occasionally hear someone say that psychotherapy is easy money, all we do is sit there and listen. Anybody could do that, surely? And if you're sitting through the eighth or ninth session of the day struggling to stay focused, exhausted, and really not quite sure about the detail of this client's story or struggling to remember what you did with them in session last week, then you might as well be anybody. Certainly, what you are not being is a professional psychotherapist. In order to really show up for every session a therapist needs an awake, interested mind, a heart willing to work at being present, and a strong, energetic focus. None of us are perfect, of course, but this is what we should be working towards bringing with us into the room every client session. Anything much less, particularly when we are charging good money for our services, is outrageous.

 The Key to PRESENCE is threefold: first, an ability to sustain focus and concentration; second, the willingness to slip the bonds of self and try to inhabit – albeit imperfectly and temporarily – the internal world of another; and third, genuineness – we really must feel interested, curious, alert and kind – clients will know if we don't.

STREAM 24: BRAVERY

Sometimes even to live is an act of courage.

Seneca

I was recently acting as the external examiner at another therapy training institute. On several pieces of student work, one of the markers was arguing passionately that students must respect the clients' feelings and should not be probing too deeply into matters which the client had not specifically raised. At first glance, this sounds uncontroversial. Naturally, we must respect the clients' feelings. My worry with this kind of mindset, person-centred needless to say, is that it implies that we dare not challenge the client, and must be extremely cautious about trying to gain insight into any of their blind spots or help them to challenge their defences, or look at those places where they are very stuck in life or don't have the knowledge or the experience to help themselves move forward. Is it really helpful to totally respect every feeling that the client brings in if they include deep levels of self-hatred, feeling lost or being in deep despair? In that marker's mind respecting this feeling seems to mean feeling that they're OK, do not need changing, and certainly should not be placed into focus by the therapist. It suggests we should wait for the client to get there in their own time.

At times, this approach can seem a bit like the blind leading the blind through a dark, sticky and very deep swamp. If the client has been struggling with these patterns of living, stuck with the same anxiety demons, suffered through decades of depression or been haunted for years by the relived trauma and frozen terrors of abusive childhoods – glibly repeating the mantra 'that the client is the expert in their own lives' doesn't quite cut the mustard for me. Person-centred theory holds this idea as part of its basic philosophy. It is well meant and in some ways is true – the client has lived their life as them for their whole lifetime; in that sense they know what it is to be them better than you or anyone else. And yet if they have been stuck in panic disorder or OCD or depression or volatile relational patterns for years, they clearly need some assistance in changing things. By the time they arrive in therapy many people are exhausted, feeling helpless or ground down. Offering assistance from a place of some particular knowledge and experience need not mean 'imposing our own agenda' or 'depriving the client of opportunities for growth' or any of the other worries person-centred therapy (PCT) practice has.

Especially in the early stages of therapy the client needs us to be something of a guide, just as the small child initially needs the parents. The aim is to support them through the process whereby they can internalise these skills sets for themselves; become the conscious and creative authors of their own lives, skilled in boundary management, self-regulation and pre-frontal cortex executive functioning; in essence to become excellent parents to themselves.

All this does not mean that we tell them where to go or deprive them of their own wisdom or agency. Rather, it simply acknowledges that we have walked through the territory of the mind and heart, and similar struggles many times before. It means that if the client is stuck in a swamp we don't act as if they are perfectly all right where they are, or merely watch as they struggle to get out themselves, we don't dive right in to rescue them either: none of these is appropriate. We assist and guide and encourage them, helping where needed and trusting their capacity to do it for themselves wherever we can. I always say to our students that it is frequently our job to name the elephant in the room. Clients sometimes need explicit permission to begin delving into more difficult territory, particularly if those issues evoke pain, shame or embarrassment. They may need us to normalise for them that this is what takes place within the therapy setting: that this is a space in which the unspeakable can be spoken.

To remind myself of this I keep a small bejewelled ornament of an elephant in my consulting room. It sits on a small table, just in my eye line, to remind me to check in on any powerful energies in the room unacknowledged or unspoken by either me or the client. These could be split off feelings of shame or rage, dissociated emotion that I am picking up which is presently unavailable to the client's conscious mind, unfinished business within the therapy dynamic and so on. I am not saying here that as soon as I notice the presence of the elephant I should name it immediately. Timing and sensitivity is the key here. However, I will usually run it through my own mind that if I'm sitting waiting for the client to name the elephant we could have a very long wait. More often than not, it is my job to gently draw attention to this elephantine presence within the therapeutic space. Most clients seem to find the fact that I take this role upon myself as something of a relief.

Reflection Point

BRAVERY

- *What forms of bravery do you admire in other people?*
- *Have you ever been able to act that bravely in your own life?*
- *Is bravery something innate to us or is it a decision we make when under pressure?*
- *How do you go about encouraging someone scared to be braver?*

Let's look at some specific situations where therapist bravery is called for: secondary gains and unconscious contracts. Some clients seem to stay stuck in the same painful situation for a very long time. Why is this? A classic example would be somebody who maintains a long-standing mental, emotional or physical illness, which hurts them and distresses them to a great degree which they feel unable to shift: say severe obsessive-compulsive disorder, panic disorder, phobias or long-term depression.

Clients in distress often communicate their enormous sense of helplessness at their inability to change. A great deal of sympathy and empathy is usually elicited from those around them; other people feel sorry for their situation. The key to understanding somebody who fits this pattern is to look for the secondary gains. This means that even when on the surface level they have been hurt badly by the psychological patterns, underneath there are secret gains for themselves which they feel unable to give up. Take someone housebound, medicated and on benefits for many years. If they 'get better' they will be faced with a series of adult tasks which require responsibility, hard work and in which they may imagine themselves as getting little support, attention or sympathy from anyone else.

The Streams in the Consulting Room

BRAVERY
Every client will have specific things that scare them: things they avoid or deny. You may have to be brave in naming them and encouraging them to face their fears.

You may need to be brave in bearing transferential anger or disappointment or resisting the need to be constantly liked or wanting to rescue.

It also takes bravery to journey with someone into their shadow side – bearing getting close to rage, grief, shame or terror that may lie behind people's social masks and psychological defences.

This can mean that in the unconscious mind the prospect of real change feels overwhelming and frightening. Remaining habitually stuck in destructive old patterns is often observed in people with eating disorders, weight issues, drug, alcohol and other addictive patterns of behaviour, many anxiety disorders, low self-esteem issues and, of course, depression. This means the therapist needs to look out for the secondary gains currently driving this person on a deeper psychological level.

The secondary gain may be attention, support, what feels like love, money or sympathy. We could describe these as mainly positive secondary gains. However, there is also a category of negative secondary gains. In this case, the game is really avoiding something which the client may fear as a result of fundamental change. In imagining change, they may see themselves as having to do things they do not want to do, taking adult responsibility, being consciously aware of the consequences of their own actions. In most cases, the driver underneath negative secondary gains will be fear. Imagine a person standing on a stone in the middle of a stormy river. Standing on the stone may have been making them miserably uncomfortable. There are several other stones around them, which at first glance may seem to be leading them towards the safety of the riverbank. However, to the person stuck in this particular mind-frame the grass is never greener on the other side. They operate using the maxim 'Better the devil you know'. This group of people tend to be very good at imagining the full catastrophe and then acting as though the disaster movie in their mind is already true. To move on the client needs to increase their conscious awareness of how the various secondary gains work in their own case. This raising of the conscious awareness is the first step towards making different choices and towards letting go of these old habits and patterns. Addressing these is hard; clients often resist and the timing and manner in which such issues can be raised must be sensitive, non-punitive and supportive. This is where the therapist needs the bravery stream the most.

A very close ally of the above issue concerns the matter of unconscious contracts. Often when I explain this to clients it's as though a light has gone on in their mind. They find the idea quite revolutionary, as I did myself when it was introduced to me around 20 years ago. I realised I'd been making many unconscious contracts with other people my whole life. It also struck me just how unhappy these unconscious contracts were often making me.

So let's explain. Let's take the example of Tamsin, a young woman originally from New Zealand in her mid-twenties who came to see me for long-lasting depression, problems with her weight and some very unhappy memories from a difficult and occasionally violent childhood. Her older brother Sean had been very bullying, mean and sometimes physically abusive from when Tamsin was nine to the age of around 18. She tried everything to placate Sean, including keeping secrets from her mother, giving him money and even apologising following altercations where he had physically injured her. Bear in mind that Sean was five years older than his sister. Over this difficult period Tamsin made one of those amazing survival decisions we sometimes take in childhood. In her case it went something like this: if I do what other people want and don't challenge them, they will be nice to me, leave me alone and not hurt me. If I put up with the maltreatment for long enough and don't do anything to provoke him eventually he will realise how cruel he is being and change his ways. Now most adults can immediately see the built-in errors here. If we are always passive and compliant towards others it is harder to challenge them when they do things which upset and hurt us. We may be more likely to be taken for a ride and the survival decision also fatally misunderstands the motivation of this increasingly sadistic brother: he may be enjoying his cruelty, revelling in the power and control he has over his little sister, feeling clever as he has managed to get her to collude in keeping his behaviour secret from their parents. Tamsin's essential decency and innocent hopefulness were acting against her in this terrible scenario. She needed somebody else to help her see what she couldn't become aware of for herself at that time.

Sadly for Tamsin it took most of the rest of her childhood and adolescence to realise this. When I met her she had been running this unconscious contract with the key people in her life for the last 15 years. When the contract was broken, which of course it frequently was, she would get very angry, upset, hurt and resentful. To her child the contract was very reasonable: if she stuck to her side then everybody else should stick to their side too. The awful truth is that there was no such contract with the rest of the world: it was an unconscious one made in her own mind and not communicated to other people. As far as everyone else was concerned there was no contract, and they certainly didn't realise that in her mind, she had bound them to this contract dipped in blood. Ultimately she needed to learn to defend herself, stand her own ground, to hold cleaner boundaries and not silently endure maltreatment by others whilst believing that they will change of their own accord eventually.

The secret to challenging unconscious contracts and secondary gains is to become aware of them. We need to start honestly looking at the contracts, boundaries, negotiations and communications we have with other people. This issue tends to be central for people who see themselves as life's constant victims: hard done by, unfairly treated. Under this category are those with strong masochistic tendencies, the passive aggressive, and anyone who sees themselves as constantly getting the short end of life's stick.

To help our clients release the bravery inside them it is important that we model bravery in the room.

 The Key to BRAVERY is the embracing of risk – it may go very wrong when we push forward and we must be willing to work with the consequences. Avoiding risk at all costs is the greatest risk in reality – if we cling to the side of the pool through fear we will never learn how to really swim.

STREAM 25: CREATIVITY

You see things and you say, 'Why?' But I dream things that never were; and I say, 'Why not?'

George Bernard Shaw

In Shaw's question of 'Why not?' – we see into the heart of the dreaming, imaginative, expansive mind of the child. The young are naturally creative, as is situated practice, which is why any therapeutic endeavour which tries to stay too rigid or static – to pay too much heed to the frozen models of our forebears – is in trouble once it reaches the unpredictability of real-life terrain. Allowing ourselves to be creative in therapy space frees up the practitioner to be more alive and responsive to the fluctuating uniqueness of the person they are presently working with – to be human and more real. Giving ourselves permission to go with our creative impulses means we are open to the possibilities of each new moment and can play with the relationship as it evolves. And each spark of creative power can provide excellent tools and tips for the well. Certain processes, descriptions, metaphors or images that catch an aspect of human lived experience perfectly can be re-used at appropriate moments. Or creatively working with physical space or objects in a consulting room can pay huge dividends. Being more creative also makes the therapy space a more enjoyable and fertile place to be – for both parties.

Some examples:

- *Choosing by Not Choosing* – lying back in the river of life and floating along: an image frequently used with anyone who is passive or who procrastinates.

- *Taming the Anxiety Monster* – facing up to it, not running away. For some clients this monster is visualised as a lion, for others a grey cloud, or a giant whale or a pool to drown in – once visualised as separate from you it is easier to tackle.

- *Urge Surfing* – this metaphor came from a client with an eating disorder who described surfing the urge to binge rather than giving into it. It is has proved useful for clients with a whole range of issues and shows that the creative spirit in the therapeutic encounter comes as much from the client as from the therapist.

- *If It's Not Perfect – It's Ruined (Or the Jam on the White Tablecloth)* – a useful metaphor for perfectionists, people with OCD and the pessimistic. It has been used to explore the polarised relationship with perfection that some people have.

- *The Box of Tricks* – a physical box I encourage some clients to use where they place objects, images, affirmations, music, stress balls, soft material – indeed anything they can use to self-soothe or self-regulate in times of emotional upheaval. The act of deciding 'I am going to go to my Box of Tricks' seems to prove a helpful distraction from the run of negative automatic thoughts or behaviours. Male clients often prefer the idea of a 'toolbox' and one client who worked in the advertising field called it her 'storyboard options'.

- *The Cushion of Responsibility* – for people who take on too much responsibility for others or who tend towards compulsive caretaking of others. I throw a cushion from my chair onto their feet without saying why. It is extraordinary how many people will continue the session with it sitting there or will simply move it to one side or pick it up and place it on their own chair. When discussed, people with this personality trait often find it tough to tell me to take my own cushion back – even when prompted. This then becomes a very useful metaphor for identifying other 'cushions' in life and how to work on getting others to take care of their own soft furnishings!

- *The Light Switch Trigger* – sometimes clients get stuck in blaming others for the pressure they put on them or for being unkind or manipulative or not respecting boundaries. The world will sometimes not treat us well – the only thing we can do in those circumstances is to work on the way we react to these triggers. One day in session a client was struggling to get this idea so I stood up and switched the light on and off. I explained that we believe the reason the light goes on is because we have flicked the switch. That is partly true – but the real reason is because the wires behind the switch are connected to the light fitting. We cannot stop others from pressing our lights switches but we can work on disconnecting our internal wiring so that the shock is more manageable. I have used this metaphor – easy to demonstrate in session – many times in the years since and it gets the point across well.

- *The Elephant in the Room* – this metaphor is used so often that it has become clichéd. However, that which is unspoken or unaddressed often lies heavy on the consulting room, being felt energetically by both parties and deeply unresolved. I feel it is the therapist's job to try to gently focus on any elephants present and bring them into the room. As already mentioned, my small jewelled elephant sits there quietly in my line of sight and often reminds me to check internally as to what is lying unsaid or avoided in the therapy today.

- *The Mummy–Daddy Dartboard* – giving space for both blame and understanding. Clients who had broadly healthy childhoods will often find it hard to accept that the way their parents related to them may have had quite negative shaping effects on their personality. Some will get quite upset – especially if the parents have died – and say 'but my mum (or dad) was lovely and they really tried hard to do their best.' All of which is undoubtedly true. However their highly anxious personality/gambling/agoraphobia/drinking/coldness/critical nature/feeling they preferred my sister to me/perfectionism etc. will have affected the young child. It doesn't make them bad people – but they are not perfect. The image of the mummy–daddy dartboard in the room allows us to throw any well-deserved darts their way (from the child's perspective) but then sometimes remove the darts from the more adult compassionate viewpoint. It gives permission to the child's woundedness whilst honouring the genuine love and gratitude they may feel for their parents. I usually add that I have my own dartboard for my parents that took me years (and lots of therapy) to fully understand.

> ### Reflection Point
>
> **CREATIVITY**
>
> - *Fear of getting things wrong is usually the reason why we block our creative flow as therapists.*
> - *Inherent in the act of creativity is trying something new – and built into anything fresh is risk; it might go horribly wrong.*
> - *Responsiveness to the changing territory we are engaging with is vital to being successfully situated and that demands our creative co-operation with the space.*

Marks-Tarlow (2012) highlights the use of guided imagery in therapy work, which I have also used to great effect many times. She points out that the use of imagery of mountains or climbing versus those of going down into basements or caves 'provides a topographical metaphor for the psyche that likens qualities of height with conscious accessibility and depth with unconscious, subcortical reaches' (p.180). The human mind enjoys creative and symbolic play and discovery whether in dream states, guided imagery, role play, drawing or parts work. These areas represent some of the most fertile ways a therapist has of assisting a client to explore embedded memories, fears, fantasies or trauma and to work through, release and transform the energy bound up in them.

The Streams in the Consulting Room

CREATIVITY

Every piece of therapy work will get stuck, feel bogged down or lost from time to time. Sometimes this is fine – maybe the client needs to circle around and return to the same dynamics, relational issues or painful memories repeatedly in order to work through them.

However, most practitioners also realise such psychological swamps are not always therapeutic – sometimes they are merely swamps with both parties slowly sinking into the quicksand.

I try to be honest about this when I feel it is happening – rather than defensive. If the client is feeling it too then I encourage us both to don our creativity caps and brainstorm around our next steps. This runs counter to the notion of being the 'expert' that many therapists cling to at all costs. Irvin Yalom calls them our 'magic feathers'. Some clients desperately want to believe we have these feathers too.

Yet we are not magicians, nor mind-readers – we too struggle and get stuck in our lives at times and sharing this with our clients helps to forge the real relationship and opens a fertile, shared and energised space which usually proves highly productive.

The creativity stream is where the arts, play, drama, dance and music therapies have a real advantage over the straight talking cure. They enable both parties to be free to explore feelings, movements, body memories, split-off terrors and unconscious defensive tactics without restriction. Creativity is closely linked to the embodiment, play and improvisation streams – and these four taken together form a good description of children when they are absorbed in activity and the inner child when they are empowered. Despite being engaged in serious and very grown-up work during psychotherapy and counselling there is no reason to block the free, spontaneous and powerful child within ourselves and our clients. The inner children frequently produce something brilliant which unlocks movement which the intellectual, sensible adult brain has been struggling to reach.

The Key to CREATIVITY is freedom – letting go of expectation and the grasping for safety and cautiousness which society sometimes teaches us – and immersing ourselves in the expansive, energetic and magical zone of playful exploration to which we all had the key as small children. This key tends to slip from our grasp as we grow up and the complex pressures of adult life bear down on us. By being creative in therapy space we model something for our clients which they can use to transform their lives.

CHAPTER 5
RIP TIDES

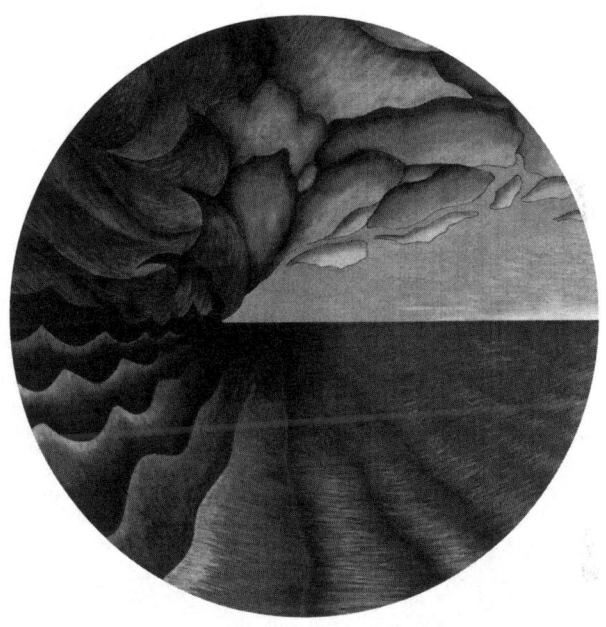

- Struggle
- Balance
- Wholeness
- Power
- Morality
- Difference
- Complexity

One reason why therapists and counsellors need the special equipment we just looked at is because when swimming in the choppy waters of therapeutic practice (just like every other part of life) we occasionally come across rip tides that can threaten to pull us under for good. They are like potentially lethal holes in the road on a journey, we cannot wholly avoid them if we wish to reach our destination but being forewarned is definitely to be forearmed. If we know there are pitfalls ahead we can learn to work with this set of streams rather than be tripped up or drowned by them, which is what tends to happen if we try to deny or avoid them which newer therapists sometimes do. These streams speak to those aspects of being with other human beings which frequently go wrong or throw up seemingly impossible dilemmas – here be dragons, in fact – but in looking them full in the face and finding our bravery we can make these dragons our servants instead of our enemies.

STREAM 26: STRUGGLE

The individual has always had to struggle to keep from being overwhelmed by the tribe. If you try it, you will be lonely often, and sometimes frightened. But no price is too high to pay for the priviledge of owning yourself.

Friedrich Nietzsche

Struggle comes with the territory

Why should struggle be one of the streams of situatedness? It makes the whole process sound a bit gloomy and difficult, doesn't it? Perhaps it does to those who are uninitiated. Think back to why models are so seductive. They make a very clever promise: come to me and I will save you from the hard work, the wrong turnings, the moments of doubt, being racked with uncertainty, the loneliness of the walk. Who wouldn't be seduced by such promises? They are, for sure, very tempting. However, as we have said, from a situated viewpoint they are mainly lies rather than promises. They consist mostly of politician's promises – the shortcut, quick fix, buy-now-pay-later mentality which has the world in so much trouble these days.

Think back for a moment to the main achievements of your life so far. If I were to ask you to write a narrative account of your experiences in getting to the point where that achievement was made manifest it would probably contain many moments – perhaps extended periods – when you doubted yourself, your abilities, your interest or commitment, worried about whether you were on the right path at all. And that will have proved very discouraging, you may have agonised over whether to stop and try something else. Many times you may have actually walked away and done something different. Was it the right decision? It's hard to know. None of us wants to strive and sweat to reach the top of the ladder only to find out it has been up against the wrong wall all along.

> Reflection Point
>
> **STRUGGLE**
>
> - *Freud's Pleasure Principle (1920) says that humans tend to avoid pain and attempt to maximise pleasure.*
> - *Is this true for you? Has it changed as you have grown older?*
> - *Think back on the key struggles in your own life and write down how they have changed you.*
> - *Was the struggle necessary to get where you needed to be? Would there have been another way through that was free of the pain?*

It is precisely at those moments of self-doubt (or doubt about the path you are walking – and one can look very much like the other at times) that we are likely to give up, move on, accept defeat or decide that something is not for us. It's too hard, I'll never get this, there are too many obstacles in my way, it's impossible. This is, of course, doubly true for somebody new to a particular piece of terrain. We look at those much more experienced in the landscape than us and think to ourselves, 'I will never be like them; they are so skilled, so accomplished and knowledgeable. They know what they are doing and what they are talking about. Look at me in comparison, so confused, so unsure! It's hopeless. Perhaps I should give up.' How easy it is to fall prey to such thinking. Someone on the first step of the ladder looks to their friend on the twelfth step and marvels at the breadth of their vision, how much they can see. What they don't see is what it may have taken their friend to climb all of those steps.

Student Excerpt
My journey across the course has proved to me that conscious knowledge is a million miles away from intrinsic wisdom that comes from experience. I have been raised to value and appreciate my senses and I know the importance of entering into a situation without preconceptions. So why did my experience of this module feel like I was discovering my senses for the first time? Because I was. I had never before looked at an abstract painting without interpretation or concentrated on how my experience of relating to people was altered when visual information is absent.

When you look at experienced practitioners in any field the years of trial and error, learning, failing and starting again, self-doubt and insecurity are invisible to your eyes. Success mainly rests in choosing not to give up when you feel like it. Anyone succeeding in any discipline will tell you that their achievements did not come easily. They will have had many times when they truly felt they could not carry on and had to give up. In those times something inside them, or maybe support from outside, enabled them to carry on a little further. One of the greatest secrets of success is that most people stop travelling down a particular road if it gets hard enough, or is too difficult too many times. Those that reach the end have somehow managed to ignore the tiredness, the doubt, the aching, bleeding feet and found some determination inside them to carry on. We must be able to bear the pain, the mistakes and the crushing blows to our self-confidence when they come and be able to step back, put them into some context and keep our vision focused on the wider landscape. The rut in the road that just tripped us and threw us off balance might prove to be an essential learning experience. Or it may simply be a caution to walk a different route next time.

> ### The Streams in the Consulting Room
>
> **STRUGGLE**
>
> One thing I have noticed in my years of practice is that many clients are passionate believers in the 'quick fix'. The modern world sells us the notion that if we find the right product, person or piece of technical kit we can find a shortcut to where we want to be that avoids pain, effort or the slow process of learning.
>
> The younger the person is the more fixed in this fantasy they tend to be.
>
> One of our secondary functions as therapists – in my view – is to help clients accept the existential truth around struggle – it is unavoidable. The first noble truth of Buddhism is *dukkha* (suffering, anxiety, unsatisfactoriness are part of life). The mature psyche recognises this and resolves to participate in these feelings with awareness rather than fearful avoidance, to open ourselves to the growth and learning they contain.
>
> So much pain is caused by attempting to defend against these existential truths – as Carl Jung said, 'neurosis is always a substitute for legitimate suffering' (1985, para. 81).
>
> We must help our clients to face these unpalatable truths – the givens of existence – just as we try to unflinchingly face them ourselves.

Every therapist will have times in counselling when they say the wrong thing, offer an interpretation that later feels way off the mark, feels disconnected, lacks focus or energy or merely struggles to connect with the unique, inner, emotional world of this particular client. Even after many years of practice there are days when one feels discouraged and questions whether what we are doing is helpful or right. We will all have sessions where we walk away feeling deskilled or unqualified to help. And moments of total chaos, mess and sadness in our own personal life where we feel how do I dare offer myself to someone else in a helping, healing capacity when I am still so wounded myself?

The growing therapist inside us must be able to survive these periods of struggle, slippage and loss. The good within us must be able to contain and soothe the bad. That is part of what we model for our clients. The containing, responding, attuned other we try to offer constantly during therapy is not the whole story of who we are. It is effortful work to maintain that quality of presence session after session but we attempt it, in much the same way as a loving parent does, because we know that a particular way of being with this person can help to heal and repair their earlier developmental wounds. It is crucial that our well contains this understanding for we will need to hold on to it very firmly in the tough moments.

Encountering your own pain

Throughout training and ongoing practice we are required to look at our own childhoods, our own personalities, prejudices, idiosyncrasies and emotional responses, partly so we are sufficiently aware of them to try to bracket them off when we are with clients. But also to understand ourselves better as part of preparing for becoming the best therapist we can. We must undertake an inner journey to the heart of self and understand its dilemmas, its terrors and its reliefs so that we can empathise with the clients we walk with on their own journey into self. Their journey will, naturally, be different from our own. We all possess a beautifully unique internal world, personal to us and shaped by our particular histories – and yet the core human experiences of anxiety, love, longing, loss, shame, anxiety, sadness, belonging, abandonment, need, hope and fulfilment are feelings that we can recognise in another if we recognise them in ourselves. They remain true across cultures, genders, ages and religions and form a bridge into the internal psyche of people fundamentally different from ourselves. They are the common food of life which all human beings taste along the way.

The struggle is part of the process towards craftsmanship. It must be embraced and utilised rather than avoided or resisted. Our struggles contain many gifts to us and to our clients which cannot be gained any other way. This is where the idea of the *wounded healer* really comes into its own. The African-American social reformer and writer Fredrick Douglas, having escaped from slavery, said: 'If there is no struggle there is no progress' (1985, p.204). In other words we learn very little on easy street.

Most clients (and most of us) will have faced hard times: this is when the adult 'project' of world mastery through the ego's expansion hits the rocks and sinks. Perhaps illness strikes or a relationship is collapsing; perhaps redundancy threatens, financial collapse, maybe the arrival of a new baby, a blow to self-image or the death of a parent. Maybe simply the onward grind of adult living with its accompanying ageing, loss of physical vitality and the tedium of ordinary life. This often first shows up in the mid to late thirties. This is often when people come running to therapy. They have followed the rules, gained the qualifications, bought the house, forged the career, developed the relationship and consumed the products. The promised deep satisfaction and happiness still eludes them. So what now? Life becomes, at some profound level, unsure and terrifying. This will usually present as stress or anxiety or depression – but the awareness of the void underneath the busyness of living has struck and it is hitting hard. This is what Yalom (1989) refers to as 'existence pain'. And it is about the worst pain there is.

Shipwreck in the adult is more far-reaching than early disillusionment in the child, because the adult has nowhere else to go, little more to hope for. The child can still hope beyond the bleakness that invades their world prematurely, deferring their happiness and fulfilment to some far-off adult life, but the adult in ruination has no compensation; they can only run away by regressing to childhood, going backwards, since if they try to continue going forwards, by looking the future in the face, all they see is a vast and profound nothing. The older one is, the more true this can become as the past keeps getting bigger at the expense of the future.

The deeps of existence intrude, invade, undermine – suddenly the existential moment of awakening arrives, and the real growing up into adulthood, through embracing what reality actually is, arrives. At this point, the adult is in a state where, to borrow the fairy tale metaphor, 'the cupboard is bare'. This is the advent of the adult who is confronted with a severe either/or: find a new way to be an adult, or continue falling into the abyss. We would contend that the situated therapist, who has lived a similar struggle within themselves, is in a good place to meet such a person when they come to therapy.

A former client of mine, Serena is in her late thirties with two children and an errant husband who has deceived her and 'let her down' many times. She comes from a family with an alcoholic mother and a partially present, often abandoning father. Her life survival strategy has been one we call 'the detective' whose inner narrative and belief system go something like this: 'If I check up on my husband thoroughly and often enough I can prevent anything bad from happening, I can stop the unexpected monster from coming round the corner and getting me. If I work at this with real diligence I can prevent life from hurting me.' It is a child's fantasy of control over the uncontrollable. It seeks to tame life, making it predictable, safe, docile and unthreatening. Sadly it stems from a child's very limited understanding of how the world works. Life is many things but predictable and controllable it is not. As adults we may know this. But at seven or five or eleven we are still terrified by such a notion and have to construct an inner world which denies this fundamental truth. The fairy story must have a neat and happy ending. Everything must turn out perfectly all right for the hero or heroine.

As for many of us, Serena has found it agonising to begin to relinquish this defensive fantasy. She has a profoundly symbiotic personality style in that she finds her sense of safety, security and comfort in life through the illusion that the presence of the other (whether this is husband, mother or her children) can be 100 per cent guaranteed if only she tries hard enough. When this illusion fails, as it often does, she is devastated and punishes herself for not having seen the change coming, for not anticipating the betrayal. At this point her sense of self begins to fragment and she descends into panic. As a child only the return of her mother could save her from this place. Now, in adulthood, she does not know how to save herself.

Our work in therapy has been to gradually encourage the terrified child inside her to accept that no perfect person will ever arrive and save her from change, uncertainty, anxiety or struggle. This is what Irvin Yalom (1989) calls being 'Love's Executioner'. In other words, nothing can save her from life itself. The fantasy that she can find such a person is hard to put down and there is much grieving to be done. She is starting to realise that she must find ways to feel safe in her own skin and accept that life can never be wholly free of risk, loss and emotional pain. As an adult she cannot hand that task wholly over to others without paying a great price. The danger of models for the practitioner is much the same. We cannot allow ourselves to fall for the comforting, yet crazy, idea that models save us from undergoing the terrors and struggles of the journey; nor can they offer the prize of hard-won wisdom gathered as a result of our walking.

The Key to STRUGGLE is mature acceptance – life is hard and painful as well as joyful and fun. Trying to evade the givens of existence: *death, meaninglessness, freedom and aloneness* (Yalom 2001) both delays our experience of the pain and intensifies it in that giving up defences created to hide from life's arrows is itself intensely painful and difficult.

STREAM 27: BALANCE

> Your hand open and closes, open and closes. If it were always a fist or always stretched open, you would be paralysed. Your deepest presence is in every small contracting and expanding, the two as beautifully balanced and coordinated as birds' wings.
>
> Rumi

Balance is vital to the situated therapist, or indeed, the situated painter, poet or mother. For there is something in that word about managing the tension between love and detachment – the tension between models and practice, the map and the terrain, the inner and the outer, my experience and your experience, art and science, the male and the female. The struggle between models led and situated ways of being in the world is incredibly ancient. It is reflected in the duality of day/night, sun/moon, science/faith and yin/yang. In the patriarchal, monotheistic Western belief, faith and magic, the more intuitive, 'female' ways of knowing have tended to be mocked and devalued as 'unscientific', particularly since the Enlightenment. The male supposedly values rationality, objectivity, evidence and self-control. Therefore he favours science.

Part of our journey towards truly owning our mastery and expertise is about balancing the streams of information coming from inside of me (my feeling, thoughts, beliefs and senses) against the streams that come from outside of me, essentially from others. This includes what others say, write, feel, think and do: their theories, books, explanations, directions and suggestions. Within any established field of practice these things coalesce over time into rules, traditions, structures and institutions. When you, as a new traveller, enter this field for the first time, much already exists, some of it appearing so solid, factual and correct that you feel bound to accept it as truth.

Remember, though, that what appears so solid now was once the internal experience of someone else, just as new and fresh to all of this as you are now.

It is hard to stay with this truth when the pressure is on you to prove yourself, fit in and demonstrate competence. The people already in the field may decide whether you can be accepted into their world, through exams, certificates and tests. Nevertheless, all of the pre-existing material in the field (other people's maps) will be filtered through your own subjective filter. An alchemical process will take place between the 'stuff' coming in from the field and the 'stuff' already inside your well. And remember your well can be the source of new creativity and change that one day may flow out of you and change the very field itself.

Reflection Point

BALANCE

- *Where does your present life feel most out of balance? Do you have any sense of control over how the rebalancing might work – if so, what?*
- *Look at the 'finding balance' see-saw diagram (page 188) – which of these axes work best for you and which one gives you the most trouble?*
- *Thinking about balance in brain function – do you recognise 'amygdala hijack' as something familiar, either now or in the past? If so what situations act (or acted) as the triggers?*

The Maasai chiefs from Kenya and Tanzania believe it is crucial to teach their young men training to become warriors the difference between situations which require ferocity and those which need tenderness. For them, the truer warrior knows instinctively which is which. The way this set of streams is constructed is very similar – knowing when we need to bring one stream to the fore and temporarily retire another, or to use one to balance the extremes within another. So whilst we must take The Leap of Faith we must also retain Awareness. In embracing Play and Exploration and Creativity we must stay in touch in with Maturity and Morality and be cognisant of the imbalance of Power in therapeutic relationships, otherwise our play may become reckless, solipsistic and damaging. Can we really embrace the spirit of Adventure whilst simultaneously Slowing Down?

To everything there is a season and our well – our internal toolkit – must have a suitable response to whatever shows up in the field. The three streams of Balance, Juggling and Complexity honour this reality. Anybody promising that learning to practise therapy really well – or mastering any challenging field of living – will be simple or fast is either deluded, naive or lying. The skilled practitioner can speed up where necessary but slow down at the hairpin bends, move in a heartbeat from the creative, playful inner child to the knowledgeable, holding and protective parent within, whilst keeping an eye on the observing, wondering, thoughtful adult. Luckily our brain is equipped to keep all these balls in the air at once if only we let it.

The Streams in the Consulting Room

BALANCE

Your client is unlikely to be entering therapy feeling at their most balanced.

Managing the various balancing acts explored in this stream will fall – at least initially – to you until they can recover (or develop) that capacity for themselves and the brain's plasticity will allow them to shape new neural networks which support more balanced functioning.

Many people need active support in rebalancing their own needs against the demands of others, the memories of trauma against the freedom of the future, the emotional needs of the child, adult and parent ego states within them.

Carl Jung believed that psychoanalysis was broadly an attempt to bring conscious and unconscious elements of the psyche into balance. Sigmund Freud saw the role of the ego as in balancing pleasure and pain: between the insistent desires of the id and its associated libido and the superego's requirements for painful adjustment to the strictures of adult society. We might also highlight the powerful feelings aroused within the transferential relationship versus the emotional experiences felt in regard to the real person. Effective emotional self-regulation requires a balance between the executive functioning of the brain's pre-frontal cortex, the emotion and feeling centres in the limbic system and the amygdala which (among many other functions) controls our fight–flight–freeze response in the reptilian part of the brain. People who cannot perform this balancing act effectively will tend to suffer from what Daniel Goleman (1999) calls 'amygdala hijack': where if the amygdala finds a match between the present trigger and the recorded previous experiences stored in the hippocampus it not only decides we have a fight–flight–freeze situation to deal with but effectively proceeds to 'hijack' the rational brain, so we become all animal responsiveness with little or no ability to reflect, evaluate, observe, analyse or calm our surging anger or fear.

We know this tendency leads to enormous problems with focus, interpersonal relationships, high anxiety and arousal, anger management, impulsiveness and problems self-soothing and delaying gratification. It shows up most frequently in those children with a disorganised attachment style (Main and Solomon 1990) whose parents may have disliked or even hated them, ignored or rejected them, overwhelmed, seduced, terrified or hurt them. The baby learns to experience the parent as both the source of comfort and fear and is left with an impossible problem to solve. The result is often severe dissociation, grossly exaggerated forms of maladaptive self-soothing, difficulty in trusting or relaxing around others and, in many families, learning that our primary tools in the managing and shaping of our relational world are power, threat, violence, abandonment and shaming. Harry Harlow *et al.*'s (1976) horribly unethical experiments with baby monkeys showed that a mistreated youngster will return to the same mother figure that hurt them as they have nowhere else to go to try to obtain protection and comfort.

Helping the client to develop the right balance between left and right brain; cortical, mammalian and reptilian; thinking, feeling and embodied ways of being in the world can be grounded in the right-brain to right-brain affective communication which good psychotherapy provides (Schore 2003).

There are countless polarities between which we are trying to find a healthy balance in our counselling work, including:

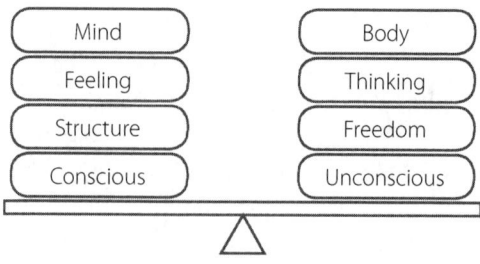

Finding balance

 The Key to BALANCE in psychotherapy is between the corrective emotional experience of the relationship which helps heal the inner child's woundedness and insight on the developmental origins and aetiology of neurosis which allows understanding and compassion for self.

STREAM 28: WHOLENESS

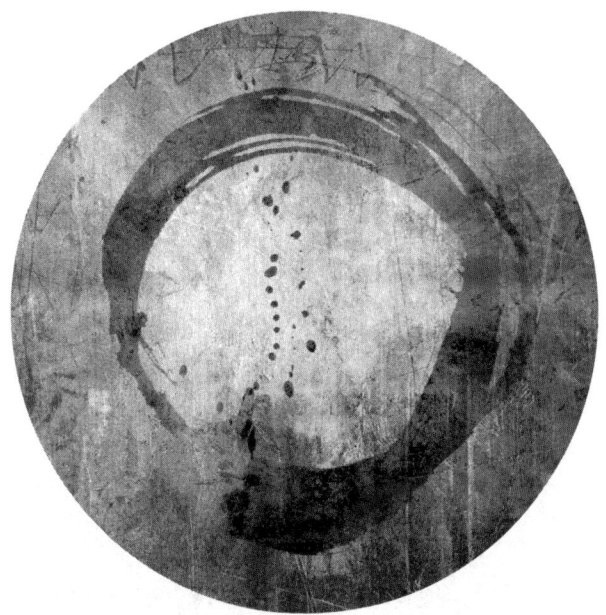

The tendency towards splitting

Splitting: The individual deals with emotional conflict or internal or external stressors by compartmentalizing opposite affect states and failing to integrate the positive and negative qualities of the self or others into cohesive images. Because ambivalent affects cannot be experienced simultaneously, more balanced views and expectations of self or others are excluded from emotional awareness. Self and object images tend to alternate between polar opposites: exclusively loving, powerful, worthy, nurturant, and kind – or exclusively bad, hateful, angry, destructive, rejecting, or worthless. (DSM–IV–TR, American Psychiatric Association 2000, p.757)

This stream of Wholeness is intimately connected to the preceding one of Balance – in fact one is not possible without the presence of the other.

Melanie Klein (1975 [1946]) was the first psychologist to utilise the term 'splitting' to explain this human tendency. As babies and young children, she argues, we have contrary experience of mother (and especially, in Kleinian terms, of her breast). Sometimes mother is 'good':

she feeds us, soothes us, smiles, she is tenderly present. Sometimes she is 'bad': she leaves us hungry or wet, is upset or annoyed, too absorbed or overwhelmed by her own interests or anxieties, or is simply not physically or emotionally with us. Klein posits that the child finds it threatening that good and bad mother may be the same person and so internally holds object relations of a separate good and bad mother. We can see in childhood fairy tales that this tendency continues.

Bruno Bettelheim, in his famous work, *The Uses of Enchantment* (1976), explains why this might be so. Because life is often bewildering the child needs chances to understand themselves in this complex world with which they must learn to cope. They must be helped to make some coherent sense out of their turmoil of feelings and need ideas on how to bring their inner house into order, and on that basis be able to create order in their life. Through the centuries (if not millennia) fairy tales came to convey overt and covert meanings, in a manner which reaches the uneducated mind of the child. In this way fairy tales carry important messages to the conscious and unconscious mind dealing with universal human problems. Stories speak to the child's budding ego and help them to relieve unconscious pressures by symbolically wrestling with terrifying thoughts and imaginings.

Reflection Point

WHOLENESS

- What do you feel when you hear the word 'wholeness' applied to human beings? To yourself?
- Think about the combination of and relationship between your mind, body, heart and soul – is one area feeling empty right now compared to the others?
- Thinking about your internal family: who is in charge most of the time – your wounded child, your nurturing parent, your rational, planning adult, your critical parent, the little professor, your free, wonder child?
- How would you like this to change?

In fairy stories evil is not without attraction – symbolised by the giant, dragon or witch, the cunning queen in *Snow White* – and often temporarily wins. The usurper may succeed for a time in seizing the place which rightfully belongs to the hero – as the wicked sisters do in *Cinderella*. In fairy tales, as in life, punishment or fear of it is only a limited deterrent to crime. The conviction that crime does not pay is a much more effective deterrent, and that is why in fairy tales the bad person always loses out. Polarisation dominates the child's mind and, therefore, must also dominate fairy tales.

In these tales a person is either good or bad, nothing in between. One brother is stupid, the other is clever. One sister is virtuous and industrious; the others are vile and lazy. One is beautiful, the others ugly. Polarities permit the child to comprehend the difference between the two.

Also these stories start to introduce the idea that one day the child must face the world without their mother and father at their side. They must grow up and separate from them, become their own individual person. To the very small child this is a terrifying thought and the stories help them to face the idea whilst resolving it safely, ideally in the presence of Mum or Dad. The child wishes and believes they will hold on to their mother eternally – the story tells us we cannot. Many fairy tales begin with the death or loss of the mother or father (*Cinderella, Snow White* – through to modern tales such as *Bambi, Finding Nemo* and the Harry Potter series). They tell the small child that if we try to escape separation anxiety and death anxiety by desperately keeping hold of our parents forever, we will only be cruelly forced out, like Hansel and Gretel, into the cold, dark forest all alone. One of the major tasks that will face this tiny person very soon is leaving whatever security they have at home and venturing out into the rough-and-tumble school world, with peers, teachers, friends and enemies, where many may like you and look after you, but some may not. We need to prepare ourselves for this quest and the bedtime stories of old are our first glimpse of a very different future world.

> ### The Streams in the Consulting Room
>
> **WHOLENESS**
>
> It is not necessary for therapists to be 'whole' all the time. I know I am not. I would be deeply suspicious of anyone who claimed they were. We are never completely fixed or healed – even if clients frequently fantasise that we are.
>
> Whilst acting in therapy space however we must strive towards wholeness within ourselves if we are to assist in the birthing process of wholeness within the client.
>
> We must be alert to the parts of them that are hiding, blocked, ashamed, too glib or too aggressive and work to understand how this part of the self fits into the whole.
>
> Always holding on to our view of the big picture whilst paying the closest attention to the tiny details of what emerges is another of the glorious paradoxes of the therapeutic task. Personally I am more of a big-picture person – sometimes finding the patience and focus needed for detail tiring and tricky. Over the years I have had to work on this – which is why Slowing Down is one of my favourite streams these days (probably because I have always found it one of the hardest to get to grips with!).

Polarities in the consulting room

In therapy this tendency towards splitting shows up all the time. For all that we may be grown up, we all demonstrate strong tendencies towards magical or wishful thinking at times. This is particularly so around romantic love. Many of us grow up believing that the perfect prince or princess will one day come and save us from the pain of living. At its most basic level this means we yearn for the arrival of a perfect object, a perfect other that will soothe us, protect us, love us unconditionally for ever and never leave. We strive to avoid the Kleinian 'depressive position' (1997 [1946]) which simply says that there is a mixture of good and bad in everything, that total perfection is a fantasy. We are all a complex amalgam of darkness and light. That includes me, you, our mothers, our lovers, our best friends, our children, our heroes and villains, murderers and saviours, the wildly popular and the brutally despised.

At some level most adults know this. And yet our fantasies, and our need to split, keep us hanging on for the arrival of the perfect other. If this girl has disappointed me then the next one will be perfect, if this man has let me down the next one will be different; the next holiday, the next city, the next purchase, the next job will be the one that brings the elusive and longed-for permanent happiness. The perfect moment is thus forever postponed, around the next corner, just visible over the crest of the next hill – maybe next time, one day my prince will come; as Morrissey sang 'please, please, please let me get what I want'. Our need to believe that perfection will arrive one day is extraordinarily powerful and letting go of it fiendishly tough.

This is why Irvin Yalom (1989) calls himself 'Love's Executioner'. Not because he is trying to kill love but rather because he has the sometimes sad task of helping clients to see that the perfect other is a fantasy that can never come true. In order to reach true maturity and, paradoxically, in order to free us to love well, we must accept this. Or we are doomed to begin searching anew each time the inevitable imperfections show up in someone or something we once saw as perfection itself. Some people will spend their lifetime wandering from partner to partner, job to job, city to city – always being enraptured at first, then disillusioned, and finally leaving with the dream of the next perfection bubbling away. They are doomed to eternal disappointment, wandering always in a scorching desert, running hard towards the oasis of their dreams only to see it vanish in the heat haze just after they get there. For them a little bad leads not to acceptance of the imperfection of everything but the renewed frenzy to start again and find the pot of gold this time. A touch of bad can ruin a much greater good. You may well recognise this type of perfectionism in yourself or others around you.

For the situated practitioner this is a valuable lesson. On first arriving in new territory we are very prone to falling in love with a model which promises to explain everything, to free us from the struggle and hard work of personal discovery. But just as the perfect mother or the perfect lover is a fantasy, so too is the perfect model. It does not exist.

Recognising the need to strive for wholeness – to avoid the destabilising swing between the extremes of polarities – is the only sure way to remain centred in your own truth whilst drawing the best from others.

The devil is in the detail – but so is the divine.

 The Key to WHOLENESS is humility and patience. Much like peak experiences of self-actualisation we may get flashes of wholeness more often than the permanent article. No matter – it is always a work in progress for both us and our clients. Pieces of the tapestry may be slowly and lovingly repaired only for new sections to unexpectedly unravel. Such is life – which is why courage and resilience are required. We can never fool ourselves that there is nothing left to learn.

STREAM 29: POWER

Nearly all men can stand adversity, but if you want to test a man's character, give him power.

Abraham Lincoln

Power and influence are two enormous issues within the psychotherapy process. Some models tend to overplay the importance of the power imbalance between therapist and client whilst others seriously underplay it. For example, classical psychoanalysis encouraged practitioners to place themselves in the role of the aloof, blank expert. The patient was the passive person, upon whom interpretations were placed. The psychoanalyst was definitely in charge, and their word was more or less final. The humanistic movement of the 1950s and 1960s, particularly in its form of person-centred therapy, as outlined by Carl Rogers (1961), tried very hard to avoid these particular pitfalls. They believed in employing the three core conditions (congruence, empathy and unconditional positive regard) and believed above all that we should try to balance out the power differential between therapist and client. After all, we are both human beings struggling to live in the world and who is to say that one of us is any better than the other. Many person-centred therapists still put forward the idea that the client is the expert in their own lives, and it's really down to us to follow them, reflecting back what they're saying to us, and to allow them to process their material in order that they can become more self-actualised.

To my mind, both of these theoretical orientations have got something right, but also something very wrong. To have an entrenched and wide power differential between therapist and client which is never acknowledged, never changes, and is not open to challenge can mean that the role of the therapist becomes incredibly self-sealing and the client ceases to exist as a real person, simply becoming a vehicle through which we can exercise our theoretical cleverness. The worst of the person-centred approach, on the other hand, can mean that the client is never challenged, that we never accept that we may have some expert knowledge that could successfully guide the person through a very difficult time.

If we look at another relationship that has some similarities to the client–therapist dyad we may find some useful instruction. I am speaking, of course, of the relationship between parent and child. One model of parenting, which we might call the Victorian authoritarian model, believes that children should be seen and not heard, follow rules and instructions to the letter and that the will or difficult spirit of the child needs to be broken, in order that the word of the mother or the father remains as law. I'm sure I do not need to outline how damaging this can be to the self-esteem, confidence and the emotional well-being of the child. On the other hand, the parallel parents to the person-centred therapists may encourage the child to be very creative, forceful and to do their own thing; however, where they tend to be weaker is that they find it difficult to enforce boundaries, discipline or insist that the child deals with the consequences of their own behaviour. Likewise, the child can sometimes miss out on a greater level of experience and knowledge that their parents, in theory, as a grown adult, should possess. In other words, these parents are too soft, too easy a pushover and the child never receives some of the strong holding, shaping and yes, discipline, that we all need in our first few years of life.

> ### Reflection Point
>
> **POWER**
>
> - In which areas of your own life do you feel the most personal power?
> - Where do you have the experience of feeling relatively powerless?
> - Who held the most power in your family of origin? How did their power make you feel when you were a child?
> - Are there particular types of people or certain situational dynamics that tend to unnerve you around issues of power? Why do you think that is?

Both the Victorian autocrat and the liberal *laissez-faire* parents could learn a good deal from one another. And by taking a few steps towards a more central position they would be doing their children a world of good. Kohut (1981) refers to this as 'optimal frustration'. In any area of life, when we are learning something new or trying to progress, we need to be optimally frustrated in order to progress satisfactorily. We need some support, understanding and guidance from those who are more powerful, older and wiser than us and at the same time we also need a chance to stand on our own two feet and fail occasionally, if we are to learn from our mistakes and take responsibility for ourselves. If we get no help at all, we are likely to struggle; on the other hand, if somebody does everything for us we are likely to remain in a fairly infantilised position and may develop the belief that the world owes us a living, sadly a position that we see all too often these days.

I try to adopt this position of optimal frustration in my role as a therapist and also in my role as a university lecturer. It is crucial that the therapist tries to see things from the client's point of view, and remains open to the idea that their interpretations or understanding about what is happening to the client may be off the mark or even completely wrong. It is also important that a warm, real relationship is created whereby trust can enable the client to explore vulnerable places and move on to some growth. However, particularly at the beginning of the relationship, we should also accept that we will have specialised knowledge and understanding that the client does not. We are performing a teaching role alongside that of a counsellor role, repairing some of the psychological gaps or wounds they carry with them from childhood. Some models seem to be afraid of this idea, but I do not see why we should be. So we should always use our power in the best interests of the client, but we must remain incredibly watchful that we never abuse it, in case our ego takes over from our compassion as the main driving force within the therapy.

> ### The Streams in the Consulting Room
>
> **POWER**
> We need to pay close attention to how this client experienced power dynamics in their childhood: was it used to scare or control them, to support and protect them or did its appearance signify emotional chaos, violence or overwhelming conflict? Was the child able to learn how to exercise their own personal power in a balanced way – or did it become squashed out of existence, or tend towards the sadistic and cruel?
>
> Likewise we must note how power operates in their present life: at work, in relationships, with children or with authority?
>
> In parallel to this we must have developed awareness of our power patterns – both childhood and present – so we understand how we affect the power dynamics in the therapeutic relationship and can use them positively rather than to reinforce traumatic experiences for the person we are working with.

We are not there to control clients or impose a worldview upon them. However, in being professionally trained and qualified we should have the qualities of an excellent guide. Although we have not walked through their particular landscape or territory before, we have walked through many others and learned something valuable in the process, which we offer to this person as a way of assisting them to find their own way more successfully through this territory.

> The Key to POWER is to temper its use with subtlety, humility and awareness. It is so easy to abuse when we are not conscious of its impact – and so easy to get lost if we deny its existence. Power is like a knife – life enhancing when skilfully used in the hands of a surgeon; deadly when wielded in the hands of an assailant.

STREAM 30: MORALITY

Nothing is at last sacred but the integrity of your own mind.

Ralph Waldo Emerson

In my private practice recently I had a fairly new client, Matt, who had been away on holiday for two weeks.

Despite the fact that my payment terms, for holidays, cancellations and the like are laid out on my website and in my written material, Matt was clearly unsure as to what the exact rules were. At the end of the first session back he offered me both the fee for that week, plus the extra fee for the two weeks he had been away. Now some psychotherapy practitioners do charge for such absences. I don't. What prevented me from simply pocketing that extra two weeks' worth of money? I guess it could partly be fear. If I had taken the money and the client had gone on to read the website a little more carefully he might have had some rather awkward questions for me the following week. However that risk was probably small. This man worked in the banking field in the City of London. There was something in the energy with which he offered the money that suggested he was not short of ready cash.

I think I handed it back to him because of the basic morality I try to bring to my work with clients. In this case it turned out that beneath the successful exterior was a man who was terrified of provoking disapproval or anger in others. He would often disadvantage himself simply in order to keep others on side. Matt feared anger and abandonment more than anything else as a result of his early family dynamics. With hindsight it may well be that he was trying to do something of this kind with me, either consciously or unconsciously, in offering to pay for the holiday sessions.

My active decision in the moment did not spring from quickly totting up the risk of being caught; it came rather from inside the well. My conception of what I am doing with clients includes trying to facilitate processes and experiences that heal them, that might repair some original childhood wounding, that I will not seek to gain something for myself to their detriment, that I will not cheat them or be dishonest with them as far as I am able. I acknowledge the power gap between us and that this leaves them in a relatively vulnerable position. It is part of my job not to take advantage of this power gap, in much the same way as a good parent will endeavour to put the needs of their child first.

That is part of the moral contract I have set up with myself in becoming a counselling psychologist. This may, or may not, mean that I would act in such a morally 'clean' way when I am not inhabiting that role. Whilst practising I hold myself to higher standards in my action than I need to outside. My needs are clearly secondary in a way that they often are not in real life. So if I had accepted that money my view of myself as a practitioner would have been radically changed even if there had been no unfortunate comeback from the client.

For me it is very important for the therapy practitioner to have engaged in this type of moral argument with themselves and to be clear in their own mind about what constitutes moral practice for them (just as it is for the doctor, the barrister, the nurse or the police officer). All professions have regulatory bodies which try to set out such moral guidelines. They normally have committees which will assess any complaints from clients about malpractice. If a psychologist is found to have breached these codes in a serious way, they can be struck off and denied a licence to practise.

> ## Reflection Point
>
> ### MORALITY
>
> - *Your personal morality in life is different from the moral framework that you must adopt when working with clients.*
>
> - *We need to hold ourselves to a higher standard than we may do at other times. The tiny deceptions, lies and avoidances that we employ to smooth our path through ordinary relationships and situations will not wash in the therapy setting.*
>
> - *Write down a list of the moral values that you try to hold yourself to in therapy space – or if you have yet to practise imagine what they might be and what may be the problems or obstacles you will face in trying to hold yourself to them.*

However the majority of challenges to our moral framework are very unlikely ever to reach the ears of an ethical committee. We must make the decisions around those alone, and reflect on them afterwards, alone, and with colleagues in supervision. At some level the choices and decisions I make around client boundary issues must sit right with me if I am to respect my practitioner self. There is something here about integrity and being able to trust yourself in your professional role. This concept of morality in practice is one of the first things which the situated practitioner needs to get in place. In many ways it is part of the platform on which the other stances and engines of situatedness are built.

The statement of what true morality is starts with the honest, brave, generous, humble, patient and respectful acknowledgment that the problem of human existence is hard. It cannot be suppressed, evaded, risen above. It has to be engaged. It has to be committed to. It has to be accepted and suffered; there is no way out of it. There is only a way through. Authentic values help us find, and walk, that way.

Sadly the world today is full of amoral behaviour – the values of the sociopath and the sadist often rule the roost in business, politics and media. These controlling, cruel and avoidant means of being with other human beings also dominate in some families too. Even in less damaged family dynamics we frequently see evasion, denial, subterfuge, manipulation and defensiveness. Therapeutic space – and the central relationship that shapes it – must exemplify a different way of being together: more honest, open, compassionate and real, acknowledging mistakes and the shadow world of emotions – anger, shame, anxiety and sadness. This is the morality of authenticity that we must strive to embody.

The Key to MORALITY is rigorous self-examination and questioning. Did I make the right decision? Or did I avoid something important because I was lazy, scared, embarrassed or putting my needs above those of the client?

STREAM 31: DIFFERENCE

> He who is different from me does not impoverish me – he enriches me. Our unity is constituted in something higher than ourselves – in Man... For no man seeks to hear his own echo, or to find his reflection in the glass.
>
> Antoine de Saint-Exupéry

Working with difference is one of the most exciting and yet challenging aspects of therapy work. Whether it's something visually obvious, like gender, race, age or physical size or something more hidden like relationships status, beliefs, family background or class, when teaching students on this topic, I often begin by saying to them that, because each of us is different, and has a unique internal world shaped by a unique family story and developmental dynamics, we are always working with difference, even if at a superficial level we have much in common with our client. It can be positively dangerous to assume that because we share certain group memberships, we show the same experiences and feelings.

So at one level we are always trying to enter a different psychological space from our own. Sometimes though, the differences between therapist and client are palpable and clear. Initially they may make us (or the client) deeply uncomfortable. The very fact of such discomfort may also disturb us. Most of us drawn to the world of therapy are caring, decent people who genuinely want to help others in distress. We may be vehemently anti-racist and anti-sexist, deplore homophobia and ageism and believe in equality and that every human being is fundamentally entitled to the same treatment. And yet – there may be aspects of an encounter with difference that we find arousing, upsetting or challenging that we were not expecting. We may find moral judgement creeping in, or distaste or repulsion. These are not easy feelings to deal with in a therapy setting – especially for those still in training taught to cultivate compassion, unconditional positive regard and empathy.

Reflection Point

DIFFERENCE

- In what ways have you ever felt different in your life? Within your family? At school? In wider society? Within your friendship circle? Now?
- Has this sense of difference been largely a source of pain or has it made you feel special – maybe both?
- Have there been times when you wish that difference wasn't there? How did you imagine you would feel if it was gone or not so visible to others?

Therapists in training often report trying to minimise the sense of difference in an attempt to equalise the power balance between them and the client. Or they report feeling somewhat embarrassed by addressing certain differences, particularly if they come from a majority group and the client comes from a minority group. Usually this is from the best of motives, feeling inadequate themselves to understand the client experience or not wanting to put pressure or embarrassment on the client. All of this comes from this assumption within ourselves of course, unlike any other assumptions we make in therapy. It's always wise to check out with the client whether we've come to the right conclusion.

I learned this very early on in training when I was working with a lady called Mary at an HIV organisation. Mary was a refugee from West Africa, whose husband had been arrested over political matters, and who had subsequently been raped at a police station, contracted HIV and had no choice but to leave two children behind in the care of her mother when she sought asylum in the UK. Initially I was very nervous as to whether I would be able to help this woman. How could I possibly understand what she had been through? Would it not be easier to have somebody from an African background to empathise with this particular client? And, most importantly of all, how was Mary feeling having to talk about such sensitive issues in front of a white man, raised in the UK?

After working for several sessions, Mary was being fairly quiet one day, and this set of thoughts was playing on my mind. Luckily I found the courage to put the question to her. She laughed and responded immediately, saying that she had been very relieved when she was allocated a white counsellor. The stigma of being HIV within the refugee community was still huge, and she was worried the news of her status would leak out if she'd been working with a black or African counsellor. My assumptions about what was going on in her mind were completely wrong.

These days, if there is a clear difference between us I try to make sure that I name it fairly early on in work. Recently I began working with a lady in her mid-seventies. I am currently in my late forties. I knew from the initial assessment that she had lost a baby as a young woman, back in the early 1960s. This was around the time I was born. So at two levels my presence as her therapist could have been provoking some deep feeling. First, because many of her issues were to do with ageing and the growing awareness of her own mortality. Secondly, because the baby boy, had he lived, would have been roughly my age. Eventually I asked Grace how it felt working with a therapist my age. At first, she was very polite, as most clients are, and said it made no difference to her at all. After a little gentle digging, however, she said that it had reminded her of the son she had lost and she'd been curious to know in what year I was born. Eventually I disclosed this to Grace, and we were able to use these feelings as a platform for a much deeper exploration of these old, calcified feelings of grief.

The Streams in the Consulting Room

DIFFERENCE

Most of us claim to be at ease with difference. It is politically correct to do so. Any discourse voicing unease with the difference of others is frowned upon. The truth is most human beings have mixed feelings around difference. We may be curious, excited, stimulated and enlivened by it whilst still having residual feelings of threat, anxiety, judgement or anger. With one type of difference we may be fully relaxed whilst another brings out the very worst in us.

All these feelings are likely to emerge in the countertransference in therapy. Pretending that the darker side is not there is unlikely to be helpful. We must be willing to explore our fear or unfamiliarity, embrace our judgements and examine their validity and above all be patient – we tend to be at our most uncomfortable with difference when dealing with people on a surface level. The deeper we go the more we tend to see of the common humanity which binds and connects us rather than the gulf of difference that may separate us.

When I was still training – and practising in a prison setting – many of the uncomfortable feelings outlined above would haunt me and even cause me to wonder whether I was made of the 'right stuff' to be a good therapist. Luckily for me I had an incredibly wise and wonderful supervisor who introduced me to the idea of 'separating the person from the behaviour'. Even working with paedophiles, rapists, murderers and arsonists I could feel much clearer about profoundly disagreeing with some of their actions – even being repulsed, angered or frightened by them – whilst still retaining some connection to the human being in front of me who had made such dark choices.

There is no one you cannot love (at some level) if you hear enough of their story. If there is I haven't worked with them yet.

The Key to DIFFERENCE is – very simply – empathy. If I can get in touch with those times in my life when I have felt teased, shut out, unfairly judged, misunderstood or vilified because of something different about me – it becomes easier to extend that understanding and empathic attunement to another. Ultimately empathy is an act of imagination carried out with a loving purpose behind it – we can learn to become better at this even if the place we temporarily imagine ourselves into is not somewhere we would choose to stay.

STREAM 32: COMPLEXITY

> I would not give a fig for the simplicity this side of complexity, but I would give my life for the simplicity on the other side of complexity.
>
> Oliver Wendell Holmes

There are so many levels of complexity within the therapeutic encounter. Trying to deal with these and stay present with your client (or even to stay sane) is frequently very tough for training therapists. For instance, trying to decide just how many people are present in the therapy room is a little like the old religious debates about how many angels can dance on the head of a pin. In physical terms, of course, there are just the two of you, unless you are working in a couples, group therapy or systemic context. From a psychological standpoint, however, things get much more complicated.

Let's start with the children in the room – the inner children. If, as a basic, we accept that each of us has a wonder child and a wounded child carried within us (see the Inner Child stream for a reminder of this) we can add two extra people onto each side: two for the client, two for the therapist. In reality, inner child work is rarely this simplistic, as there may have been several points during the developmental process when clients were blocked or repressed or when they had to edit their personalities in some way. We may meet several sub-personalities or parts of the self, which represent the client at age four, eight and 15 and carry very particular psychological baggage. And whilst this is true for them, it is also true for us. Let's now take a look at the parents present: first, the client's mother and father. Even if this person did not grow up with their mother or father there will still be a fantasised or wished-for parent present in the room. That's two more people for the client side. We also have to add our own parents, of course. From the countertransferential perspective, our parents also make themselves known, at times during the therapy process. And no parent is one-dimensional. So the loving, seductive, chaotic, critical or distant elements of those people will leak out into the process itself too. We are rapidly running out of chairs. Current or former partners of the client will also have a strong psychological presence in the room as will anybody that has left a very deep mark on us emotionally. We can add to this: siblings (if we have them), children (if we have them – or our feelings about the children we do not have), influential work colleagues, bosses and teachers, friends and enemies. In fact, the more you look at it, the more crowded the room becomes. And for the therapists we also have influential teachers and supervisors, their own previous therapists, particular founding fathers or mothers of their preferred models – plus their partners, children and so on. Luckily all these people are not present physically otherwise our sessions would need to be held in the Albert Hall. And yet the fact that we cannot see them does not mean they are absent psychologically, emotionally, spiritually or intellectually. So we cannot ignore their vital role in shaping the process, the relational space or the internal emotional world of the client or the counsellor, our defensive structures, blind spots, idiosyncrasies, fears and fantasies.

The smart therapist recognises that we are working in a packed room and that there is wisdom in this crowd as well as trouble; that this multitude of invisible presences must be taken note of, felt, talked about and acknowledged.

> ### The Streams in the Consulting Room
>
> **COMPLEXITY**
>
> In this stream I use the metaphor of the *fighter pilot* (see page 211). It's a great metaphor but it can never do justice to the lived experience of the real thing. Real-world territory usually demands fast reactions and throws up unexpected twists and turns when we least expect them, it throws us off balance. Learning to roll with such rapidly changing conditions takes time and boundless compassion for the self.
>
> If a self-critical voice within is too omnipresent – we will never find the space inside ourselves to learn, grow and develop.
>
> Therapy space is a paradox – packed with multiple layers of meaning, feeling, memory and unexpressed emotion, suffused with the body and its storehouse of reaction, traumatic residue and yearning, full of relational dynamics and their fantasies and fears – and yet, at heart, it can feel like the purest, simplest, most honest space in the world.
>
> We should not ignore the complexity present but never forget the underlying simplicity and beauty of human connectedness and being that lies beneath and beyond it.

Another central element of complexity is the ongoing debate about how many aspects there are to the therapeutic relationship itself. Whole books have been written about this. And, naturally, like most other psychotherapy/counselling phenomena no two therapists can truly agree about it. In the lectures I give at university on this topic I generally rely on the five relationship model, developed by Petruska Clarkson (2003). Many theoretical models tend to have a dominant focus on just one or two aspects of the therapeutic relationship. It's probably fair to say that most therapists practising today accept that to focus too heavily on one element of the therapy relationship, whilst ignoring others, only gives us part of the overall picture.

Even the most basic counselling contract needs a solid working alliance in place. The alliance gives a platform on which any other therapeutic activity can rest. It means that the two parties involved understand and agree to certain basic rules and to stay within certain basic roles. Bordin (1979) refers to basic goals, bonds and tasks which the two parties must share. The broad psychodynamic school of thought has alerted us to the importance of the transferential relationship. In a nutshell, this says that human beings carry within them a set of rules or templates for how they expect others to interact with them and how they see themselves in relationship to other people and they may carry across old emotional responses, defences or attractions into present-moment encounters, often being unaware of why they are doing so. These models are shaped through early relational experiences and are added to throughout life, sometimes becoming stuck or habitual. One can argue that they form the core of what we call the personality. Most orientations recognise some sort of process that fits this basic type. In object relations, it may be called an internalised working model of relationships, in cognitive-behavioural therapy it may be referred to as schemas or scripts, and within traditional psychoanalysis it is interpreted as transferential or projected material. In essence, all are saying much the same thing, that human beings do not come fresh to every new relational encounter. We carry with us the joys, fears and expectations developed in earlier relational contexts. From a psychodynamic perspective, the most influential of these contexts will come from the first seven or so years of life, with the dominant figures of mother and father looming large.

Reflection Point

COMPLEXITY

- *How complex is your present life? When you contemplate that complexity what feelings emerge?*
- *How does your body react?*
- *For many of us modern life produces feelings of being overwhelmed as we drown in ever more complicated layers of information, duties, caring roles and the never-ending administration of life.*
- *How do you manage the complicated tasks of your life? How did your parents' role model that for you? Do you feel their lives were simpler than your own?*
- *Think of someone whose life seems more simple to you – do you have feelings of envy, pity, sadness or joy?*

The third relational aspect referred to by Clarkson is the reparative or reparenting element (or the developmentally needed relationship). This idea emerged initially within the British School of Object Relations and the American School of Interpersonal Psychology, with themes connected to how we relate to other people. Harry Stack Sullivan (1953) exemplified this when he described the core need of human beings (from infancy to old age) as being for 'interpersonal security' (p.45) – thus rejecting the central premise of Freudian drive theory.

If parts of our personality had to go underground, in order to feel safe during childhood, to feel accepted, wanted, worth something or simply to ensure our physical survival, we may carry some deep wounds or places where it feels broken or shut down. On the other hand, certain other elements of the self may have been pushed to the front of the stage, if that made the people around us happier, less upset or angry or more likely to give us the kind of emotional nurturance we needed. We may have learned to be quiet, compliant, or to always say yes to someone more forceful than ourselves, so that they let us stick around. Our inner clown may have learned to be funny and self-deprecating so that people like us. Or we may have come to the conclusion that the only way to get ourselves heard was to be angry and violent. The reparative relationship within therapy therefore seeks to use relationship to help heal these wounds and to give these lost parts of the self a chance to re-emerge in an environment where they are welcomed, valued and supported.

The two remaining relationships that Clarkson points to are the real relationship and the transpersonal relationship. The real relationship speaks to that element of the contact between therapist and client, which comes from outside of our respective roles. It is those lovely moments of human-to-human meeting, something referred to by Martin Buber (1923) as the 'I–Thou' relationship. Incidentally, it is the real relationship that seems to be very highly prized by clients themselves. Clearly this is more likely to emerge in the longer-term pieces of work, in a four or six-week contract there is limited time and space for such a relationship to evolve. The final one of the five is the transpersonal relationship. In some ways it is the most controversial. It certainly refers to things which are traditionally seen as outside of the scientific realm. We may call it religion, spirituality or the personal belief system, but to many clients it is of central importance in their lives – and to some therapists too of course.

The *fighter pilot* is a metaphor that I originally came up with to describe how I felt at times during therapy sessions when I was still training. I remember in very early sessions trying to pay close attention to my body, sitting in a very open position, using good eye contact and trying to be aware of voice tone. At the time I was also trying to learn the various key psychotherapy models. Depending on which books I had read and which lectures I had attended that week, my focus might have been pulled in a more psychodynamic direction, towards Gestalt, or I might have been trying to embody the Rogerian core conditions. I would also remind myself to keep an eye out for transferential material. Then again, what about countertransference? Were the feelings I was having in response to the client's material really about them? Or was it triggering feelings and memories from my own unconscious mind? Was this material getting in the way of me doing a good job? Then again, maybe these feelings were just straightforward empathy, the result of trying to enter into the client's world and get some understanding of what it might be like to be them. It was also possible that I was completely off track and what I was dealing with here was more in the field of Kleinian projective identification! With this mass of plates already spinning in my crowded mind, was I paying sufficient attention to which aspects of the therapeutic relationship were currently being expressed in the room? Had I sufficiently built a strong enough working alliance? Were we in a reparative phase? Was there some profound transpersonal element taking place that I was completely blind to?

I recall trying to explain what this felt like in a supervision group. The best description I could come up with was that of a fighter pilot during World War II, under fire from enemy planes, and yet still trying to pay attention to the multiple streams of information in the cockpit of the plane I was flying: so many dials in front of me recording height, speed, air pressure and altitude, yet with one eye on where my crosshairs were focusing and thinking about when to fire. And all the while feeling a terrible responsibility for the other people on board the plane with me, fearing the whole thing might run off track and crash at any moment. If it was complicated enough in the 1940s, I would imagine any pilot flying a modern plane has to pay attention to even more streams of information coming into their mind at top speed. One may assume that in this modern technological world we may be very used to living in the midst of such information overload. However, to my mind, it takes a good deal of practice and experience to reach the point where one can assimilate all of these competing and powerful streams of emotional, non-verbal and intellectual information whilst still retaining a basically attuned emotional presence with the client – being in what I referred to earlier as absorbed in optimal flow.

As with any other complex set of skills which have been performed over years or decades, the really wise and experienced therapist will make it all look terribly easy. And yet we must allow ourselves to grow and assimilate the skills over time. Nobody can get to this point of deep experience overnight, it simply isn't possible. The trick at the beginning is to gradually open up one's perception to ever more complex layers of feeling and connection within the intersubjective therapeutic space. Including ourselves, with such permission, we can begin the journey of moving from trainee pilot to expert flier.

 The Key to COMPLEXITY is – ironically – simplicity. Getting too caught up in the complexity of things leads to burn-out, overload and disillusionment – it is part of why many clients come to see us in the first place. Whilst acknowledging the complex nature of life and learning to work well within it we must always try to hold on to the simplicity of every human heart with its needs for belonging, love, warmth, safety, meaning and connection.

CHAPTER 6
PRACTISED WISDOM

- Maturity
- Craftsmanship

These last two streams encapsulate everything that has gone before. We are back to the 10,000-hour rule that I mentioned at the beginning (see page 15). Achieving and living from this state of practice wisdom takes real time. Like fine wine there is a fermentation process that happens inside the well that one day will begin to produce something closer to vintage wine rather than simple water. Often by this stage the practitioner is guiding others in their journey as well as working with their own clients: as teachers, lecturers, training supervisors, researching, writing, presenting at conferences and workshops – passing on something of the embodied and hard-won practical wisdom they have forged along the way, acting as a guide and mentor to the next generation of eager, naive, excited and terrified travellers.

STREAM 33: MATURITY

To exist is to change, to change is to mature, to mature is to go on creating oneself endlessly.

Henri Bergson

Accepting our experience is not simply a matter of owning our subjectivity, as if it could exist hermetically sealed in and cut off from all else, but rather is a matter of owning the intersubjectivity that allows everything to influence us, and us to influence it.

Look at the faces of older people who have reached some wisdom and you will see the blows etched on their face, but in someone who has weathered this, seen it through, rather than fleeing it, these very rents are marks of dignity, beauty, strength and compassion. They embody survival and endurance. Compare these faces with the vacuous, shiny, pretty pleasantness of the people used in advertising; the pinned-up smiles are masks over emptiness and far from being persuasive, the happiness suggested is shallow and empty. Such faces convey a living that is 'above it all', or 'out of it', and thus lacks both the gravitas and understanding that remaining with experience bestows. Shallowness and vanity versus depth and gravitas is what we are considering in this stream.

Schopenhauer (2000) in *The World as Will and Representation* notes that in almost all languages the etymological root of the words describing vanity – in Latin *vanitas* – originally meant 'emptiness' or 'nothingness' (p.205). To fill up the well of the wise practitioner with water that is both practical and meaningful we must strive to leave vanity and surface behind. Another stream considered for this book was Humility (but I had to draw the line somewhere). The end product of having walked through territory 10,000 times cannot be mainly driven by vanity, ego, superiority or disdain for those less experienced. Compassion, empathy and love cannot spring from such brittle and rocky ground.

The therapist going through the motions, feeling more ennui and resignation in meeting a new client than curiosity and tenderness, must surely ask themselves some serious questions about whether it is time to do something different. The wonderful writer and therapist Dorothy Rowe once gave a very honest newspaper interview (2002) in which she talked about why she had given up practising as a therapist.

> Working as a therapist is a tremendous responsibility because you interfere in people's lives. I don't see clients anymore because you get to a point where you feel you're not doing your work very well. There aren't many new plots in people's lives and when someone starts to tell you a story and you know how it's going to turn out then you stop really listening properly.

This shows a real professional being honest with herself about where she is on her journey and acting on her awareness in the best interests of both her clients and herself. I also know of practitioners still working in their seventies and eighties who are as enthusiastic and passionate about their client work now as they were 30 years ago – we are all different.

> ### Reflection Point
>
> **MATURITY**
>
> - *Do you feel like a mature person? Really?*
> - *Try to access the parts of you that still feel small, unsure, playful, silly and spiteful, and just want someone else to do it!*
> - *We tend to add layers of maturity around this core – and naturally what I consider mature behaviour may be seen by you as the height of immaturity.*
> - *Even the best of us dip in and out most of the time – if what we mean by maturity is responsibility, selflessness, thinking through consequences, delaying gratification, working hard – I don't know anybody who personifies those qualities 100 per cent of the time. Actually I wouldn't want to – they wouldn't be much fun to hang out with!*

Mature working within therapy is a matter of the therapist appreciating, from within their own experience, the personally different yet humanly common experience of the client. The therapist's job is to stay with the emerging energy of the client, paying close attention to what they are experiencing to help reveal the blocks, and sore points, of the client's energy. This, in turn, enables the therapist to direct the client's attention to their own experience, and to facilitate an exploration of it. The therapist must not be overpowered, seduced or terrified of the client's energy, surrendering to its neurotic demands by colluding, avoiding, refusing to challenge where needed or stand their ground when they must. Neither can the therapist take up the opposite posture and simply observe and interpret the client, at a safe, clinical, uninvolved distance, refusing to experientially feel the client or connect deeply with their individuality.

Many people never outgrow the child. The wounded, defended, adapted part of their psyche stays in charge long after they are living in an adult body. The parts of the self that experienced arrested development are easily triggered in the present day, and the acting out, projection and denial of negatively charged transferential material creates a never-ending parade of new psychodrama, conflict, self-loathing or damage to others. They may demand 'primitive merger' with lovers, unconsciously use their own children as security blankets and block that child's own individuation-separation process, or they may compulsively repeat the same tired scripts of anxiety, depression, relational tension and existential avoidance. These are people who still long for life scenarios with 'happy ever after' endings, and the like, angry and frustrated that life is not constantly happy, fulfilling, entertaining and indulgent. Letting go of the child's fantasies and defensive positions is tough but necessary if we are to genuinely grow up and become an adult. Mourning the loss of the perfect object – the perfect me, the perfect life – is part of the work of therapy.

But what are the adult's consolations for losing the fortunate child's lot of protection, safety and relative ease? These are more to do with the ego: ambition, triumph, success, public display of one's power and status. This does not demand merger or happy endings or refuse to enter adult power games, but it too relies on certain psychological and behavioural crutches. Existence must be a puzzle that can be solved by sufficient effort, intelligence and power. The illusion that sustains the adult's ego is 'power over' fate, and therefore the capacity to create one's own destiny out of one's own forcefulness. The child's evasive myths are of one kind, the adult's evasive myths of another.

In either case, existential reality is shut out. If the child must give up dewy-eyed romanticism, the adult must give up hard-boiled scepticism, or existential reality remains held at a very long arm's length. The child fantasises being in the arms of benign powers, like adoring parents; the adult fantasises the ego as a tough guy, standing alone, capable of blasting through every obstacle and overcoming every challenge.

Letting the adult's consolations die is horrendously difficult, and few people do it. This is why Irvin Yalom (1989) refers to himself as 'Love's Executioner'. He does not mean it is his job to kill all love, thankfully. Rather to kill the need for the adult to believe in 'the perfect object' to come and rescue them, the prince, or princess, who will come from over the horizon and end their aloneness, that feeling of being misunderstood or not held. In many adult lives that fantasised rescuer can show up as friend, child or hero as well as the more obvious form of lover or partner. Such relatively mature adults may not need merger and happy endings, but they need predictable order and reliable control, they need measurement of outcomes, they need the definiteness that puts everything in neat and tidy boxes, or they cannot 'play the game'. Some adults just follow the rules that are pre-set, and some adults play the game to win even if they have to stretch the rules. This is why models will always have their seductive powers until we get wise to them. Yalom (1989, p.13) says that all therapists must be able to tolerate and work with a great deal of uncertainty. This quotation sums up the approach to situated functioning brilliantly:

> the public may believe that therapists guide patients systematically and sure-handedly through predictable stages of therapy to a foreknown goal, but such is rarely the case: instead...therapists frequently wobble, improvise and grope for direction. The powerful temptation to achieve certainty through embracing an ideological school and a tight therapeutic system is treacherous: such belief may block the uncertain and spontaneous encounter necessary for effective therapy. (1989, p.13)

Between Chaos and Clarity

Part of what changes over time as a therapy practitioner is your relationship to chaos, the unknown and anxiety. When we begin our journey towards experience or craftsmanship, in any sphere of activity, we are often seen as 'green', and we usually feel very green too. The canvas in front of us is largely blank, the world is full of exciting freedom and possibility yet concurrently drenched by gripping fear, anxiety and the terror of failing, being found out, getting it all wrong. These are the feelings outlined earlier in the book in my account of a first ever therapy session and in the first few sets of streams.

In other words, the majority of the field is unknown to you. All you have are the accounts of others who have journeyed in the field before you and come back with their theories, models and ideas (frozen in time) of what the field is like. And to most human beings a great expanse of the unknown is always a little terrifying, even as it may pump us full of adrenaline and generate the excitement of anticipating what is about to come. The situated approach to activity is to embrace that period of chaos and the treasure trove of understanding it can produce. It is not, however, good to stay in that place for ever – it is not a place of wisdom. As we journey into the field more and more, we start to build up (in our well) a plethora of experiences, responses, knowledge and memory. It is like being dropped down in the middle of an unknown city and getting 50 chances to walk in different directions. On each of those visits you will have learned some of the topography of this place. You will know that this street can lead on to this alley or if you double back it will take you towards the train station. You will have walked down the same street three times and hit a dead end. You will have experienced that magical moment when turning an unexpected corner led you to witness the most beautiful open vista across town.

Now the experienced practitioner faces a profound challenge: how to move along the spectrum from chaos to clarity, from the known to the unknown, all depending on where you may be with a particular client, and not cling to one end. So each time you encounter a schizoid client you will know something about what it feels like to live in the schizoid neighbourhood of town. To an extent you will know your way about. However, you don't know what it feels like to be this particular person having lived this particular life. That is, and always will be, new to you and you need to take the time to find out. You must not be tempted to miss the exploration of the chaos and the unknown in this person's story. You may be familiar with the neighbourhood, and even the street, but you have never been inside this house before. It would be arrogant, foolish and harmful to the client, were you to assume you have. They would not feel seen, heard, understood or held in any real sense. Likewise, it would not serve the client were you to have to start from scratch all over again each time. You do retain many useful things from each trip.

The Streams in the Consulting Room

MATURITY

What to say about being a mature therapy practitioner? You know when you have it and when you don't – unless you think you have it when you actually don't – or when someone else sees it in you but you struggle to own it for yourself – or when a run of poor sessions sets you wondering whether you've lost it if you ever had it in the first place.

This sense of oneself is never a fixed, solid, permanent thing – as very little is in situated territory. Others are often able to see it before you can recognise it in yourself. It creeps up on you gradually only to slip away during some of the toughest moments.

For me the only truth of the maturity stream is to accept that it may be a frequent walking companion the longer your journey goes but it will slip away and hide at times – don't panic, accepting its impermanence is actually part of being mature.

Pema Chodron, a Buddhist nun, says in her book, *When Things Fall Apart* (2005), that much of the current mental distress in Western life is caused by people desperately trying to run at full pelt away from anything too painful, challenging, anxiety provoking or risky. She likens this to viewing a garden from behind a thickened sheet of plate glass; we yearn to see, smell and feel the garden but are terrified of anything that might bite us, prick us, dirty our clothes or make us sneeze. This sanitised way of being in the world is close to the worst excesses of models. Mature therapists (and clients) need to do everything they can to avoid it and a sustained focus on how to practise in a more situated way is one way to help us do this.

The situated therapist must strive to remain in balance, somewhere between chaos and certainty, accepting that there will be moments of both and that both have something unique to teach us. To lunge desperately for total certainty denies too much of what constitutes life itself, whilst to indulge oneself in nothing but chaos loses the wisdom and craftsmanship that is built, shaped and finessed with every new walk into the wild. The journey allows us to find the necessary love to work with our clients, whilst our training teaches us the necessary detachment.

 The Key to MATURITY is the ability to relax in therapy space and accept the highs and lows as merely part of life's rich pattern. Maturity frequently lets go of the need to control, yet is able to contain and direct when that is needed. It is balanced, flexible and honest – this stream draws upon so many of the ones that precede it and incorporates them into an extraordinary blend.

STREAM 34: CRAFTSMANSHIP

Without craftmanship inspiration is a mere reed shaken in the wind.

Johannas Brahms

What we are calling craftmanship here can be given many other names: craftmanship, mastery, artistry, expertise, brilliance or accomplishment. However we may name this phenomenon its deepest roots lie in the building of practice wisdom – ability acquired through training, discipline and experience.

This is where we all hope to end up when we begin our journey – so it is only right that craftsmanship should be the final stream in this book. No matter what you call it we all know when we see it and it makes us marvel at someone's ability to perform something so complex with seeming ease and flair. Something in us knows that they have been practising and perfecting this skill, this craft, this art – for a *very* long time. Perhaps we feel awed and inspired – maybe completely terrified and daunted if we are trying to take our first fragile steps along a similar road.

This stream is closely related to Stream 7: Slowing Down. It harks back to a time when everyone understood that to be judged as capable within your chosen field took a great deal of time. One moved from a state of apprenticeship, very gradually, to become a master craftsman. This was true for goldsmiths, weavers, carpenters, builders, stonemasons, sailors, artists, architects – any role where a body of skill, knowledge and experience had been honed, polished and tested over time to the point where that person could be said to have developed expertise. Using our established metaphor – they have a deep well, overflowing with abundant, clear water.

Student Excerpt
The most powerful and fearful aspect of situated learning is the responsibility it places on individuals and this has important ramifications in therapy. Intensive therapeutic training fails to maximise on what both client and therapist already know whereas situatedness allows the client, and counsellor, to possess the answers to their own problems deep within themselves.

There is no 'Reflection Point' box, no single key nor 'The Stream in the Consulting Room' box for this final stream. What would be the point? No few words can do justice to something so incredible. We know it when we see it precisely because it is relatively rare in this world – most people do not have the patience, determination, courage and talent to stick with a path for long enough. We should also remember that mastery of our craft is never a single destination – we can go on adding to the mix, making it richer and deeper for as long as we live. In evoking craftsmanship we can speak of beauty, grace, glory, splendour and melody; it expresses qualities that seem to take on a life of their own – flowing, impressive, fluid and powerful. Like watching an accomplished jazz pianist, a skilled carpenter or a mesmerising actress it has the capacity to move and change the world. To catch even glimpses of it within ourselves is something extraordinary – worth every painful step of the journey to get there.

Instead for this final stream I want to try to share some tips and tricks for strengthening and deepening the wellspring of craft you carry inside you – some operational rules for using the well: a kind of handbook for the well-user.

It is tempting, if rather romantic, to think of the well as some underground wellspring of knowledge and intuition flowing up unaided from our unconscious mind. Certainly Jung would have been attracted to such an interpretation of this idea. For me this is too passive, starry-eyed and simple a notion. The water in a well lies underground. It will not climb its way up the side of the well of its own accord. There is nothing magical about it. Its truth is more prosaic. It requires a human hand and human strength and human intention to make it to the surface. We must, first, be conscious of its existence. If we are not, it is of limited use to us and to others. Second, we must wind the mechanism so that the bucket lowers, captures some water and then pull it back up again. Then the water is available for us to drink, or to feed our plants or animals. We must maintain the mechanism, ensuring the rope and the bucket stay strong and the well is unblocked.

If we don't use the water in the well in an active manner, the wellspring underground dries up. Thus how we use the bucket and rope, to bring the water up, is crucial. The more actively you use the well, the more ready it is to 'flow up'; but you are still consciously and actively involved in this 'getting the water out', at least initially. In explaining this concept to our students we often extend the notion of the well to include the metaphor of the fountain for how situatedness operates in practice.

When you are in a real situation and the flow begins from the well, what is often referred to as 'getting into the zone', you will begin to find that you no longer need to be so consciously aware of reaching down into the well for decisions about action, choice of words, stories, ideas or instant reactions to changing circumstances. This is when the flowing up from the depth of the well takes on the qualities of a fountain: sparkling, bubbling up and surging out of you into the surrounding fields. It is something like taking the cork out of a bottle of champagne; it carries its own energy and momentum. It feels exciting to be the source of this energy, but it is also thrilling and inspiring to be around it too.

When you are experiencing this for yourself, in a therapy session, on a stage, a sports field or in a business presentation, it feels truly extraordinary and something quite beyond you in many ways. This is what it looks like when any craftsperson in their field gets deeply into situated being. That is when it can start to feel like something magical is happening. But the truth is that people need time to develop such capacities. The beginner may have flashes of such brilliance but they cannot be relied upon to any great extent.

So the notion of the well as simply unconscious is too limiting. In fact it operates across the unconscious and conscious spheres of our mind, both within and without of ourselves, intrapsychically and interpersonally. In other words it is truly intersubjective. Like the lungs, it takes air in from the outside, uses it, transforms it, then feeds it back again to the outside world. It is cyclical, fluid, ever changing and draws its content from a variety of sources, rather than one underground stream. That is why I often extend our central metaphor – so that in our well bucket there is not simply water, but soup: something richer, mixed with ingredients from different places that affect one another in a process of alchemy and transformation.

> I launch myself into the therapeutic relationship having a hypothesis, or a faith. That my liking, my confidence, and my understanding of the other person's inner world, will lead to a significant process of becoming. I enter the relationship not as a scientist, not as a physician who can accurately diagnose and cure, but as a person, entering into a personal relationship. Insofar as I see him only as an object, the client will tend to become only an object. I risk myself...at times this risk is very real, and is keenly experienced. I let myself go into the immediacy of the relationship where it is my total organism which takes over and is sensitive to the relationship, not simply my consciousness. I am not consciously responding in a planful or analytic way, but simply in an unreflective way to the other individual, my reaction being based on my total organismic sensitivity to this other person. (May 1991, p.54)

When people are drowning in the deep water of unknown and overwhelming experience they cry out for a model as a lifebelt, to save them. What they really need is to learn how to swim, not just to survive in the water but eventually to excel. The journey through these 34 streams, from the Leap of Faith to Craftsmanship, parallels all such learning journeys – whilst Stream 1 speaks to the scared, the unsure, the reluctant beginner within us, the craftsmanship stream speaks to the extraordinary within us: the Pablo Picasso, the Björn Borg, the Alan Turing or the Ella Fitzgerald. Few of us can sustain such heights – but we can get to the summit within each of us. People are models-hungry when in the novice state, and those who belong to models as an ego badge are only too willing to throw the drowning a lifebelt as a way of recruiting them to that model. The person flailing in the water does not realise that the lifebelt they gratefully cling to comes with a brand name on it and, sometimes, a lock without any key. They are prevented from ever learning to swim in deep waters. Fear convinces us we can never swim, and this is hijacked by true believers in models to enslave us to their structured and articulated system.

However we now know there is there is another way: developing and trusting practical wisdom. Once we have ingested the best, or most relevant, from a rough guide and its travellers' tales, this goes into the unconscious and alchemically becomes mixed in with our own personal learning direct from the terrain – this mixing of instruction with experience fills the well. Externally located support can be taken away, sometimes lets us down or can be destroyed by events; but the well is inside us and can never be taken away. Zen says, 'The Self is the real book.' As I say to my students: the contents of the well can never be left on the bus, run out of battery charge or be stolen at the pub, it becomes an essential part of you and will be with you for the rest of your days.

The Alchemical Soup

When you make a bowl of soup for the first time it is likely you will follow a recipe. Maybe the combination of ingredients is the same one your mother or grandmother used. Perhaps it is a traditional recipe where one follows fairly rigid rules. Initially you will look for guidance outside of yourself in making the soup. And you will look at the reactions of those eating it to see if it tastes good. Over time this process changes. You may adapt your cooking style, picking up tips for adding some spice or different vegetables. Your taste probably adapts over the years. In any case you probably become more skilled at preparing food and if someone coming for dinner likes things a little different you can adapt your cooking process for them; indeed you enjoy doing so, it gives you the chance to experiment. Most importantly, you are the final arbiter of whether the soup works. You taste it, smell it, and watch as it bubbles on the stove, adding a little pinch of something here and there. When we taste the finished product we are sometimes curious to know the various ingredients that formed it. But we experience them together as one delicious whole.

For me therapy is much the same. The well inside of us contains an ever-changing, ever-moving alchemical soup of ideas, theories, therapy models – the experience of others filtered – and importantly our own beliefs, joys, losses, wounds, resilience, learning and reflection. The need to separate and categorise these things out is an outgrowth of a models mindset. In the consulting room, when the well bucket dips down into the soup it captures something unique each time. Needing to chemically analyse the soup to find out how many grams of each ingredient it contains may well be an interesting exercise but is it a useful one for the experienced therapist? Not usually. Rather the wise practitioner knows that their training in particular models has provided much of the base for the soup but the things that make it special and tasty come from them.

Trusting in your own well and its contents lies at the heart of therapeutic confidence in the field. I encourage you to take on this knowing, no matter what stage of the therapy experience you are at, and be guided by it. Develop your awareness of just how rich and magnificent is your well. Learn about its continual and growing presence inside you. Intuition, trust and the ability to be present in the moment, flowing inside your own creative response to whatever the territory sends your way, will all help you to make the contents ever deeper and more complex.

And in order for the soup to be edible it must be cooked. We often refer to a therapy session as a kind of stew or soup with our students. In much of our teaching of counselling and psychotherapy we artificially separate out such phenomena as empathy, transference, countertransference, self-disclosure, reflecting, challenging and the therapeutic relationship in order to help students get a feel for them. They are necessarily taught in separate lectures. But a real therapy session is not experienced in that way, we do not finish a session and say to ourselves, well, that one was about countertransference or empathy; boundaries or self-disclosure. All of these things are happening often at the same time. Multiple streams of emotional, physiological and intellectual information are flowing through us, around us and between us throughout the session. Much like an airline pilot we have to keep our eyes on many dials and screens at the same time, which is why juggling and complexity are two of the streams. It is being able to move gracefully through this complex flow that is the main challenge.

For me, situated action is much the same. I have outlined 34 streams of situatedness which I feel are vitally important aspects of this approach to mastering any field of human activity. Yet we know that they will be experienced in the real world of territory in bunches: story and dialogue, immersion and awareness all at the same time. In any case, 34 is an arbitrary number – why stop there? By now you may be screaming at me (metaphorically) about how could I have missed out such and such?

There is no defence against such accusations – this list is partly driven by subjectivity and partly by the requirements of a relatively brief book.

So the differentiated streams are the ingredients of the soup but we taste the soup as a whole. Time acts as one of the heat sources cooking the soup – that is why the streams of the journey and slowing down are so vital to understanding the situated way of being; and why I stress, again and again, that situated action is not anti-models. Disrespecting complex terrain by pretending you can walk into it totally unprepared is naive, arrogant and in some cases, like those French mountaineers earlier in the book, possibly fatal.

If a casserole is meant to stay in the oven cooking slowly for five hours it is no good taking it out after five minutes and serving it up to your guests. It will be raw, lumpy, cold and indigestible. For the alchemy to work it needs time and heat to allow an exchange to take place between the various ingredients, for them to affect one another, be changed and transformed, to release their flavour and colour over one another and become something completely different from what they were when they were thrown into the pot. Mastering any craft or practice in life is much the same. The stuff (experiential, theoretical, anecdotal, emotional, philosophical) which goes down into the cooking pot that is the well inside you often re-emerges looking and feeling very different from how it did going in. Indeed this is why we are often surprised by something that comes to us in a moment of inspiration when we are deep inside real-world territory. Afterwards we say to ourselves, slightly shocked, 'Where on earth did that come from?' or 'I didn't know I had it in me!' And that is one of the wonderful truths of the well. We don't have to keep a running inventory of everything that it contains. We don't have to run an exhaustive administrative audit every six months. Its richness, once cooked, is there for us for the rest of our lives. We can draw upon it time after time, and yet still be delighted by some new element of it that has not been seen before.

Cream of Alchemy Soup

So not only must we be conscious and active to get the water flowing, it is also true that many of the soup's ingredients come from outside, through immersion in the terrain. As the well breathes in and breathes out we draw things in from outside, as well as tapping into latent powers from the inside. The outside and the inside cook together.

What comes in from outside? Models do, but only as sifted, digested, excreted, by us in our personal experience – and they are useful in your well when they retain that fundamental tie to the experiential ground. Abstractionist thought only serves to poison the well. Far more vital in filling the well is our relationship with clients. All that we take in, assimilate and learn from the relationship with clients adds much living water to our well.

The well does add something powerful, in creativity and inspiration, to the limits of the conscious mind. It won't do this, however, unless the conscious mind is conscious and active, in its own right. The surfer has to be a good rider of the wave, or the wave does not come.

So it is vital that we become conscious of the well's existence, how to use it, and, crucially, to trust that it will work for us in moments when we are faced with the blank space to be filled or the unexpected tiger that rounds the tree. In that sense this paradigmatic approach to therapy is encouraging conscious activity in managing one's well and its contents, rather than some wispy, fairy-tale notion of what situated practice is about. There is nothing soft about it. Whilst it questions over-dependence on models and notions of scientific objectivity it still demands discipline, rigour, courage and effort from the practitioner.

So regardless of whether you are brand new to therapy or have been practising for many years I want to encourage you to trust in your well and develop your awareness of it. Even if you are just starting out you can know that even though in your current tunnel you cannot presently see the light, you are moving towards it and it will start to appear. You must trust the process and keep walking. The aim of this concept, and this book, is to reduce overwhelming anxiety and fear in practitioners so they feel less compelled to swear blind allegiance to so-called 'evidence-based' practice and manualised approaches to therapy.

Imagine the sea and its different moods. On some days if you wish to swim you will have to deal with a tempestuous ocean. Waves will crash in and sweep you off your feet. Your head will be pushed underwater and at times you will not know which way is up. You will have to feel, or fight, your way back to the surface. On other days the sea is calmer and you swim more clearly, and with greater purpose, back toward the beach. You may feel at home in one type of water more than the other but we all have to learn to function well under both conditions, and move between them as required. Experienced therapists will do this naturally, seamlessly blending together their hard-won knowledge of the territory gained over many years walking and the confused, magical, shocking encounter with the very new. That is why balance is so important for the situated practitioner, and why this notion of the well contains a soup of so many elements.

The surface of the water gives us access to the clarity of the air; under the surface affords us experience of the deeper realm of feeling and mystery. The best therapists (or practitioners in any field) will, like the otter, the whale or the dolphin operate happily in either realm and move easily between the two. Once models have been digested in the system a person can become capable of clarity of a different kind when operating in the field (or under the water). They can take something from the land with them when they dive under the water and use it in a different way.

It was in this intersubjective arena that the child of the client was blocked, wounded, hurt or ignored. It was here that the child decided which parts of them were not acceptable, not special enough, felt unlovable or never seemed to be admired. They will have learned to deny, hate or camouflage those aspects of self that seem to anger, bore, repulse or distance them from others, which invite mockery or provoke teasing or the threat of exclusion from the group. They will have learned to feel ashamed of those parts of the self, to direct venom towards them, wish they were gone. A whole personality, and a whole lifetime, can be built upon trying to hide from the world those parts of your child self which you learned were not really wanted or good enough. And it is in this relational place (in therapy or without) that those parts may dare to come to the surface again to find some healing, some acceptance of the real self. Only then can clients take the control lever of their life out of the terrified, rageful hands of their wounded, battered child. Only then can they let go of the rigid defences of childhood which have become so maladaptive and damaging.

To be an effective witness and guide to this process, to see it, hear it, feel it, share it and shape it the therapist must be skilled, knowledgeable and wise, knowing when to step in and when to stand back, to communicate care, empathy and compassion, to be powerfully tuned in to what the person is feeling in the here and now and also to the terrors, pains, losses and confusions they may have felt as a child. To do all this well, session after session, is not easy and given that we are only flawed human beings ourselves we need support – the ideas, images and experiences shared in this book and its streams aim to be a good companion for those walking the road to mastery. I encourage you to recognise just how rich your own practical wisdom already is and to stay open to deepening it as much as you can.

> Practice is the best of all instructors.
>
> Publilius Syrus, Roman author

REFERENCES

Altheide, D. L. and Johnson, J. M. (1994) 'Criteria for assessing interpretive validity in qualitative research.' In N. K. Denzin and Y. S. Lincoln (eds) *Handbook of Qualitative Research*. Thousand Oaks, CA: Sage Publications.
American Psychiatric Association (2000) *Diagnostic and Statistical Manual of Mental Disorders, Fourth Edition*. Arlington, VA: American Psychiatric Publishing.
Anders Ericsson, K., Krampe, R. and Tesch-Romer, C. (1993) 'The role of deliberate practice in the acquisition of expert performance.' *Psychological Review 100*, 3, 363–406.
Arendt, H. (1958) *The Human Condition*. Chicago, IL: University of Chicago Press.
Aristotle (1953) *Nichomachean Ethics*. Translated by J. A. K. Thompson. London: Penguin Books.
Aristotle (1962) *The Politics*. Translated by T. A. Sinclair. London: Penguin Books.
Badenoch, B. (2008) *Being a Brain Wise Therapist*. New York, NY: Norton.
Baron-Cohen, S. (2011) *Zero Degrees of Empathy*. London: Penguin Books.
Belloc, H. (2009) 'Jim' in *Cautionary Tales for Children* (first published 1907). Copenhagen: SMK Bokks Edition.
Bettelheim, B. (1976) *The Uses of Enchantment: The Meaning and Importance of Fairy-tales*. London: Penguin Books.
Bordin, E. (1979) 'The generalisability of the psychoanalytical concept of the working alliance.' *Psychotherapy: Theory, Research and Practice 16*, 3, 252–260.
Bowlby, J. (1997) *Attachment and Loss, Volume 1*. London: Pimlico.
Buber, M. (1923) *I and Thou*. Translated by Walter Kaufmann. New York, NY: Touchstone.
Clarkson, P. (2003) *The Therapeutic Relationship*. London: Whurr Publishers.
Chodron, P. (2005) *When Things Fall Apart: Heart Advice for Difficult Times*. Shaftesbury: Element.
Cozolino, L. (2010) *The Neuroscience of Psychotherapy*. New York, NY: Norton.
Crossley, N. (1996) *Intersubjectivity: The Fabric of Social Becoming*. London: Sage Publications.
Csikszentmihalyi, M. and Csikszentmihalyi, I. (eds) (1988) *Optimal Experience: Psychological Studies of Flow in Consciousness*. Cambridge: Cambridge University Press.
Czarnomski, F. B. (1956) *The Wisdom of Winston Churchill*. London: Allen & Unwin.
Danaher, G., Schirato, T. *et al.* (2000) *Understanding Foucault*. London: Sage Publications.
De Zulueta, F. (2006) *From Pain to Violence: The Traumatic Roots of Destructiveness*. Chichester: John Wiley and Sons.
Deurzen-Smith, E. van (1988) *Existential Counselling in Practice*. London: Sage Publications.
Douglas, F. (1985) 'The Significance of Emancipation in the West Indies.' Speech. Canandiagua, New York, August 3, 1857. In Blassingame, J. W. (ed) *The Frederick Douglass Papers. Series One: Speeches, Debates and Interviews. Volume 3: 1855–63*. New Haven, CT: Yale University Press.
Ellis, Bret Easton (1998) *Glamorama*. New York, NY: Picador.
Evans, T. and Wallace, P. (2008) 'A prison within a prison? Masculinity narratives of male prisoners.' *Men and Masculinities 10*, 484.

Freud. S. (1977) *A Project for Scientific Psychology (unfinished manuscript)*, in *The Origins of Psychoanalysis: Letters to Wilhelm Fliess, Drafts, and Notes: 1887–1902* (first published 1895). New York, NY: Basic Books.

Freud. S. (2003) *Beyond the Pleasure Principle and Other Writings*. London: Penguin Modern Classics (originally published in 1920).

Gallese V., Fadiga L., Fogassi L. and Rizzolatti G. (1996) 'Action recognition in the premotor cortex.' *Brain, 119,* 593–609.

Gerhardt, S. (2004) *Why Love Matters*. Hove: Brunner Routledge.

Gibran, K. (1991) *The Prophet* (first published 1923). London: Pan Macmillan.

Gladwell, M. (2009) *Outliers: The Story of Success*. London: Penguin Books.

Goleman, D. (1999) *Working with Emotional Intelligence*. New York, NY: Bloomsbury.

Greene, R. (2012) *Mastery*. New York, NY: Penguin Books.

Harlow, H. *et al.* (1976) 'Social rehabilitation of separation-induced depressive disorders in monkeys.' *American Journal of Psychiatry 133,* 11, 1279–1285.

Hart, C. (2009) *Figure It Out! The Beginners Guide to Drawing*. London: Random House.

Hebb, D. (1949) *The Organization of Behavior*. New York, NY: Wiley.

Heidegger, M. (1962) *Being and Time* (first published 1927). Translated by J. Macquarrie and E. Robinson. Oxford: Basil Blackwell.

Henman, L. (2008) 'Humour as a coping mechanism: lessons from POWs.' *International Journal of Humour Research 14,* 1, 83–94.

Howard, A. (2000) *Philosophy for Counselling and Psychotherapy: Pythagoras to Postmodernism*. Basingstoke: Palgrave MacMillan.

Hutchins, E. (1996) 'Organizing Work by Adaptation.' In M. Cohen and L. Sproull (eds) *Organizational Learning*. London: Sage.

Jeffers. S. (2007) *Feel the Fear and Do It Anyway*. London: Vermilion.

Jung, C. G. (1955) *Modern Man in Search of a Soul* (first published 1933). New York, NY: Harvest Books.

Jung, C. G. (1985) *Collected Works, Vol 16: The Practice of Psychotherapy*. New Jersey, NJ: Princeton University Press.

Kant, I. (2007) *Second edition of the Critique of Pure Reason (Kritik der reinen Vernunft)*. London: Penguin (originally published in 1787).

Kierkegaard, S. (1945) *Fear and Trembling* (first published 1843). Translated by Alistair Hannay. London: Penguin Books

Klein, M. (1975) 'Notes on some schizoid mechanisms.' In M. Klein, *Envy and Gratitude and Other Works* (first published 1946). London: Hogarth

Klugman, D. (2001) 'Empathy's romantic dialectic: self psychology, intersubjectivity, and imagination.' *Psychoanalytic Psychology 18* (September), 4.

Koestler, A. (1989) *The Act of Creation* (first published 1964). London: Arkana New Edition.

Kohut, H. (1981) *How Does Analysis Cure?* Chicago, IL: Chicago University Press.

Kohut, H. (1977) *The Restoration of the Self*. Chicago, IL: Chicago University Press.

Lippard, L. (1997) *Six Years: The Dematerialization of the Art Object from 1966 to 1972*. Cambridge, MA: MIT Press.

Mahler, M., Pine, F. and Bergman, A. (1973) *The Psychological Birth of the Human Infant*. New York, NY: Basic Books.

Main, M. and Solomon, J. (1990) 'Procedures for identifying infants as disorganised/disorientated during the Ainsworth Strange Situation test.' In M. T. Greenberg, D. Cicchetti and E. M. Cummings (eds) *Attachment During the Pre-School Years: Theory, Research and Intervention*. Chicago, IL: University of Chicago Press.

Marcel, G. (1952) *Metaphysical Journal*. Chicago, IL: Henry Regnery.

REFERENCES

Marks-Tarlow, T. (2012) *Clinical Intuition in Psychotherapy: The Neurobiology of Embodied Response.* New York: W. W. Norton and Co.

May, R. (1965) *The Art of Counselling.* Eastbourne: Gardener Press.

May, R. (1991) *The Cry for Myth.* New York, NY: Norton.

Merleau-Ponty, M. (2013) *The Phenomenology of Perception* (first published 1945). London: Routledge.

Mitchell, S. (2000) *Relationality: From Attachment to Intersubjectivity.* London: The Analytic Press.

Montgomery, A. (2013) *Neurobiology Essentials for Clinicians.* New York, NY: Norton.

Nietzsche, F. (1969) *Thus Spake Zarathustra* (first published 1891). Translated by R. J. Hollingdale. London: Penguin Books.

O'Leary, P. (1995) *Door Number Three.* New York, NY: Tom Doherty.

Ortega y Gasset, J. (1957) *Man and People.* Translated by W. R. Trask. New York, NY: W. W. Norton.

Owen, W. (1920) *Poems with an Introduction by Siegfried Sassoon* London: Chatto & Windus.

Plath, S. (2002) *The Unabridged Journals of Sylvia Plath.* New York, NY: Anchor Books.

Polanyi, M. (2009) *The Tacit Dimension* (first published 1966). Chicago, IL: University of Chicago Press.

Polanyi, M. (1958) *Personal Knowledge: Towards a Post-Critical Philosophy.* Chicago, IL: University of Chicago Press.

Rogers, C. (2004) *On Becoming a Person* (first published 1961). London: Constable.

Rowe, D. (2002) 'This much I know', interviewed by Ursula Kenny for *The Observer*. Available at www.theguardian.com/theobserver/2002/sep/01/magazine.features7, accessed on 6 February 2015.

Rumi (1995) *The Essential Rumi.* Translated by C. Barks. San Francisco, CA: Harper.

Sanderson, C. (2013) *Counselling Skills for Working with Trauma: Healing from Child Sexual Abuse, Sexual Violence and Domestic Abuse.* London: Jessica Kingsley Publishers.

Samples, B. (1976) *Metaphoric Mind: A Celebration of Creative Consciousness.* Boston, MA: Addison Wesley Longman Publishing Co.

Schopenhauer, A. (2000) *The World as Will and Representation* (first published 1818). New York, NY: Dover Publications Inc..

Schore, A. (2012) *The Science of the Art of Psychotherapy.* New York, NY: W. W. Norton and Co.

Schore, A. (2003) *Affect Regulation and the Repair of the Self.* New York, NY: W.W. Norton & Co.

Siegel, D. J. (2012) *Pocket Guide to Interpersonal Neurobiology: An Integrative Handbook of the Mind.* New York, NY: W. W. Norton and Co.

Simon, H. A. and Chase, W. G. (1973) 'Skill in chess.' *American Scientist 61*, 394–403.

Smith, M. K. (2003) 'Michael Polanyi and tacit knowledge.' *The Encyclopedia of Informal Education.* Available at http://infed.org/mobi/michael-polanyi-and-tacit-knowledge, accessed on 6 February 2015.

Stack Sullivan, H. (1953) *The Interpersonal Theory of Psychiatry.* New York, NY: W. W. Norton and Co.

Stolorow, R. and Atwood, G. (1992) *Contexts of Being.* Hillsdale, NJ: Analytic Press.

Suchman, L. (1987) *Plans and Situated Actions: The Problem of Human–Machine Communication.* New York, NY: Cambridge University Press.

White, M. (1995) *Re-Authoring Lives: Interviews and Essays.* Adelaide, South Australia: Dulwich Centre Publications.

Winnicott, D. W. (1971) *Playing and Reality.* London: Hogarth.

Yalom, I. (2001) *The Gift of Therapy.* London: Piatkus.

Yalom, I. (1989) *Love's Executioner.* London: Penguin Books.

SUBJECT INDEX

abstractionism, of models-led theory as 33–4, 228
Act of Creation, The (Koestler) 129–30
alchemical soup 225–8
amygdala hijack 187
Angst 61–2
anticipatory anxiety 153
anxiety 49–50, 58–9, 61, 153
apprenticeship 16–8, 81
Aristotle 14–5, 17, 33
Art of Counselling (May) 120
attachment patterns 72, 123, 187
attunement 140–1
avenues of immersion 102

Balance (Stream 27) 184–8
beginner's mind 46–7
Being and Time (Heidegger) 67
black humour 131–2
body, Embodiment (Stream 12) 107–10
body-mind dualism 96
box of tricks 171
brain
  amygdala hijack 187
  empathic circuits within 122–3
  mirror neurons 157
  neuro-plasticity 123
  right-brain to right-brain communication 10, 119, 187
Bravery (Stream 24) 164–9
Buddhism 180
busyness of living 181–2

CBT, dominance of 119, 161
challenging the client 164–9, 195
chaos 218–20
chess, mastery in 15
children
  connecting with inner child 75–9, 78–9
  experiences in childhood 71–3, 135, 158, 229
  fairy tales 190–1
  inverted relationship with parents 158–9

play of 65, 67, 68, 69, 174
relationship with parents 70–2
reparenting the self 76–7, 209–10
wonder child 74–5
wounded child 74–5
see also Inner Child (Stream 6)
choosing by not choosing 171
Clinical Intuition in Psychotherapy (Marks-Tarlow) 118–9
cognitive immersion 113
Complexity (Stream 32) 206–12
conditions of worth 71
connecting with inner child 75–9, 78–9
consulting room 96
contract
  counselling 208–9
  unconscious 168–9
counselling contract 208–9
countertransference 106, 140
Craftsmanship (Stream 34) 221–30
creativity 67, 126, 170–6
Creativity (Stream 25) 170–6
crying 106
cushion of responsibility 171

dark humour 131–2
death anxiety 191
defence mechanisms 70, 72–3, 152
Diagnostic and Statistical Manual of Mental Disorders (DSM) 23
Dialogue (Stream 9) 91–4
Difference (Stream 31) 202–5
Digging (Stream 21) 149–54
discovery, driving force of situated action practice 33
Discovery (Stream 2) 48–52
dissociative identity disorder (DID) 78
divine paradox 54
'Dulce et Decorum Est' 28–9

Einstein, Albert 116
elephant in the room 165–6, 172
embodied writing 109–10

Embodiment (Stream 12) 107–10
empathy 120–4, 157–8
Empathy (Stream 15) 120–4
existence pain 181–2
expectation, driving force of models-led theory 33, 48
experience, learning from 14–5
Exploration, Play and (Stream 5) 65–9

fairy tales 190–1
family *see* children; mother; parents
Fangio, Juan Manuel 26–7
fantasy of perfection 192–3, 216–7
fear, facing head on 47, 59, 61
feeling 106
Feeling, Seeing, Listening (Stream 11) 102–6
female
  intuition 118
  as unscientific 184
fight, flight or freeze 49–50, 187
fighter pilot metaphor 211
first session 24–5
first-person narrative 86–90
five relationship model 208
flow 66–7
Freud, Sigmund 14, 35, 186

gender
  intuition and 118
  see also female; male
Gestalt therapy 78
Glamorama (Ellis) 112
good mirroring 71
guided imagery 173

heart, voice of the 106
Hebbian theory 50
home (as a space) 97
Human Condition, The (Arendt) 14
Humour (Stream 17) 129–33
hyper-focus 66–7
hysteria 150

I-Thou (Buber) 93–4
if it's not perfect - it's ruined 171
imagery 89–90, 171–3
immersion
  cognitive 113
  into unconscious 112
Immersion (Stream 13) 111
impatience 56–7

implicit knowledge *see* Tacit Knowledge (Stream 16)
improvisation 26, 27–8, 117, 145–8
Improvisation (Stream 20) 145–8
individuation-separation 49
influence, and power 194–7
inner child 70–9, 174, 206
Inner Child (Stream 6) 70–9
intelligence
  two kinds of 18–22
  see also well, the
interpersonal neurobiology 123–4
interpersonal space 44
interpretation of experience 87
intersubjective field 92
intersubjectivity 68, 91–2, 92, 155–9
Intersubjectivity (Stream 22) 155–9
intrapsychic space 43–4
intuition 111, 116–9
Intuition (Stream 14) 116–9

Journey, The (Stream 3) 53–7
juggling 140–4, 186
Juggling (Stream 19) 140–4
Jung, Carl 186

Kant, Immanuel 14
Knowledge, Tacit (Stream 16) 125–8

Leap of Faith (Stream 1) 41–7
  see also Immersion (Stream 13)
light switch trigger 172
limiting beliefs 153
listening 104–6
Listening, Seeing, Feeling (Stream 11) 102–6
loom, therapeutic 142
'Love's Executioner' 193, 217

magical child 74–5
male, as scientific 20, 184
Man and People (Ortega y Gasset) 91
map, abstract 33–4, 228
masochistic tendencies 169
mastery 15–8, 221–30
Mastery (Greene) 16
Maturity (Stream 33) 214–20
meaning, relationality of 92
mechanistic practice 23
Metaphor, Story and (Stream 8) 85–90
mind-body dualism 96
mirroring 134–5

models-led theory
　as abstract map 33–4, 228
　after-the-fact reconstructions 32, 35
　blocking effective practice 21, 40–2
　claims made by 22
　differences from situated-action theory 22, 31–3
　expectation is driving force 33, 48
　illusion of safety of 13–4, 34, 58, 60–1, 146, 224–5
　philosophy of 38
　quick fix approach of 81, 180
morality 121, 198–201
Morality (Stream 30) 198–201
mother
　primary empathy with 122, 156
　separation anxiety 49, 191
　splitting and 189–90
multi-tasking *see* Juggling (Stream 19)
mummy-daddy dartboard 172–3
music, mastery in 15–6, 51–2

narrative, first-person 86–90
narrative form 85–6
neuro-plasticity 123
neurobiology, interpersonal 123–4
neuroscience, mirror neurons 157

object relations theory 71, 92
objectivity, radical 156
Of the Means of Belief 24
Olivier, Laurence 29–31
optimal flow 66–7
optimal frustration 136, 196
Outliers: The Story of Success (Gladwell) 15
over-caretaking 158–9
Owen, Wilfred 28–9

pain
　encountering own 181
　existence pain 181–2
parents
　models of parenting 195
　present in the room 207
　relationship with their child 70–2
　see also mother
passive aggression 169
patience 83–4
perfection, fantasy of 192–3, 216–7
person-centred theory 71, 160, 161, 164–5, 194–5
Personal Knowledge (Polanyi) 126

personality (sub-personalities) 77–9
phronesis 14–5
Place, Space and (Stream 10) 95–9
Plato 14, 33
Play and Exploration (Stream 5) 65–9
playfulness 65–6, 68, 69
Playing and Reality (Winnicott) 69
pleasure principle (Freud) 178
Power (Stream 29) 194–7
practise
　bad habits 55, 116
　getting into the zone 55, 67, 223
practise wisdom 20–1
praxis 14–5
Presence (Stream 23) 160
professional organisations 66
'Project for a Scientific Psychology' (Freud) 119
psychoanalysis 136, 160
psychopaths 122, 155
psychosomatic illness 150

quick-fix approach of models-led theory 81, 180

radical objectivity 156
radical subjectivity 155
rationalisation of therapy 23
real relationship 210
reparative relationship 209–10
reparenting the self 76–7, 209–10
repression 151–2
resistance 84, 152
risk
　improvisation and 147–8
　working with 34, 60, 62
　see also Bravery (Stream 24)
room, consulting 96
rush, desire to 56–7, 81

safety, illusion of 13–4, 34, 58, 60–1, 146, 224–5
St Augustine 14
schizophrenia 78
science, Western 13, 19–20, 23, 118–9, 126
script, sticking to 31
secondary gains 167
seeing 103–4
Seeing, Listening, Feeling (Stream 11) 102–6
self, reparenting the 76–7, 209–10
self-story 86–90

SUBJECT INDEX

self-system 44
sensorium (counsellor's) 108
sensory knowledge 109
separation anxiety 49, 191
setting (consulting room) 96
shallowness 214
situated-action practice
   blocks to 21, 40–2
   definition 14
   differences from models-led theory 22, 31–3
   discovery is driving force 33
   philosophy of 38
   requires practice 82
   symbolised by water 38, 228–9
situatedness, definition of 21
situational awareness 27
Slowing Down (Stream 7) 80–4, 104
sophia 14–5
soup, alchemical 225–8
Space and Place (Stream 10) 95–9
splitting 189–90, 192
sticking to a script 31
story
   Story and Metaphor (Stream 8) 85–90
   see also fairy tales; narrative
Struggle (Stream 26) 177–83
sub-personalities 77–9
subjectivity *see* intersubjective field; intersubjectivity; Intersubjectivity (Stream 22); radical subjectivity
survival strategies 70, 72–3, 152
symbiotic personality style 89, 183
sympathy 121

Tacit Knowledge (Stream 16) 125–8
taming the anxiety monster 171
10,000 hours rule 15–6
therapeutic loom, the 142
therapeutic relationship 208
therapeutic space 96–7, 98–9
Thus Spake Zarathustra (Nietzsche) 46
training 63–4, 114, 151
transferential relationship 208–9
transmuting internalisations 122
transpersonal relationship 210
trust 143
tuning-in 140–1

Unabridged Journals (Plath) 137
uncertainty 217–20
unconscious contracts 168–9

uniqueness of the client 83, 89
urge surfing 171
Uses of Enchantment, The (Bettelheim) 190

vanity 214–5
victimhood 169
voice of the heart 106
vulnerability 150–1

Warmth (Stream 18) 134–9
water metaphor 38, 228–9
Weissmuller, Johnny 26
well, the 19–20, 35–6, 41, 116–7, 222–9
When Things Fall Apart (Chodron) 219–20
Wholeness (Stream 28) 189–93
William the Conqueror 27
wonder child 74–5
World as Will and Representation (Schopenhauer) 215
wounded child 74–5
wounded healer 159, 181
writing, embodied 109–10

Zero Degrees of Empathy (Baron-Cohen) 124
zone, getting into the 55, 67, 223

AUTHOR INDEX

Adler, A. 102
Altheide, D. L. 21
American Psychiatric Association 189
Anders Ericsson, K. 15
Arendt, H. 14
Aristotle 14–5, 17
Atwood, G. 92

Badenoch, B. 69, 74, 123
Baron-Cohen, S. 124
Belloc, H. 153
Benjamin, W. 145
Bergman, A. 49
Bergson, H. 214
Bettelheim, B. 190
Bordin, E. 208
Bowlby, J. 88
Brahms, J. 221
Buber, M. 23, 93, 210

Chase, W. G. 15
Chodron, P. 219
Churchill, W. 85
Clarkson, P. 208, 209
Cozolino, L. 74, 123, 158
Crossley, N. 92
Csikszentmihalyi, I. 66
Csikszentmihalyi, M. 66
Czarnomski, F. B. 85

Danaher, G. 92
De Zulueta, F. 74
Deurzen-Smith, E. van 61
Dostoevsky, F. 15
Douglas, F. 181

Ellis, B. E. 112
Emerson, R. W. 198
Evans, T. 92

Fadiga L. 157
Fogassi L. 157
Freud. S. 119

Gallese V. 157
Gerhardt, S. 123, 158
Gibran, K. 95
Gide, A. 58
Gladwell, M. 15
Goethe, J. W. van 43
Goleman, D. 187
Greene, R. 16

Harlow, H. 187
Hart, C. 134
Hebb, D. 50
Heidegger, M. 67
Henman, L. 132
Holmes, O. W. 206
Howard, A. 33
Hutchins, E. 128

Jeffers. S. 47
Jekyll, G. 149
Johnson, J. M. 21
Jung, C. G. 88, 144, 180

Kant, I. 13
Kierkegaard, S. 46, 61, 62
Kington, M. 129
Klein, M. 54, 189, 192
Klugman, D. 92
Koestler, A. 111, 129
Kohut, H. 65, 80, 121, 122, 136, 196
Krampe, R. 15

Lincoln, A. 194
Lippard, L. 98

MacDonal, G. 160
Mahler, M. 49
Main, M. 187
Marcel, G. 29, 32–3
Marks-Tarlow, T. 69, 118, 119, 173
May, R. 120, 224
Merleau-Ponty, M. 91
Mitchell, S. 92
Montgomery, A. 69, 74

Nietzsche, F. 23, 46, 107, 177

O'Leary, P. 21
Ortega y Gasset, J. 91
Owen, W. 28–9

Pine, F. 49
Plath, S. 137
Polanyi, M. 125, 126
Proust, M. 53
Publilius Syrus 230

Rizzolatti G. 157
Rogers, C. 160, 194
Rowe, D. 215
Rumi 18–9, 184

Saint-Exupéry, A. de 202
Sanderson, C. 74
Schopenhauer, A. 215
Schore, A. 119, 158, 187
Selden, J. 140
Seneca 164
Shaw, G. B. 170
Siegel, D. J. 123, 163
Simon, H. A. 15
Smiles, S. 48
Smith, M. K. 126
Solomon, J. 187
Stack Sullivan, H. 44, 209
Stein, M. 116
Stolorow, R. 92
Suchman, L. 14

Tesch-Romer, C. 15
Thoreau, H. D. 120

Wallace, P. 92
White, M. 87
Winnicott, D. W. 69, 97, 135, 156

Yalom, I. 174, 182, 183, 193, 217–8